Housing

for Low-Income

Urban Families

WORLD BANK COUNTRY ECONOMIC REPORTS

WORLD BANK RESEARCH PUBLICATIONS

WORLD BANK STAFF OCCASIONAL PAPERS

Published for the World Bank

THE JOHNS HOPKINS UNIVERSITY PRESS
BALTIMORE AND LONDON

Orville F. Grimes, Jr.

Housing for Low-Income Urban Families

Economics and Policy in the Developing World

The views and interpretations in this book are those of the author and should not be ascribed to the World Bank, to its affiliated organizations, or to any individual acting in their behalf.

Library of Congress Cataloging in Publication Data

Grimes, Orville F., Jr. 1943–
    Housing for low-income urban families.

    Bibliography: p. 159
    Includes index.
    1. Underdeveloped areas—Housing. I. Title.
HD7391.G74   301.5′4′091724   76-4934
ISBN 0-8018-1853-2 cloth
ISBN 0-8018-1854-0 paperback

Table of Contents

Tables

Figure

Preface

THIS STUDY IS A PRODUCT of the interaction among World Bank staff members and consultants much more than an individual effort. Begun by the Development Economics Department as an attempt to understand the role of housing in urban development and to find ways of reducing poverty in cities, the study was drafted in the Urban and Regional Economics Division of that department and benefited from close collaboration with the Transportation and Urban Projects Department.

At the same time three persons contributed so substantially to this work that it is impossible fully to identify their separate contributions or how they differ from mine. Helen Hughes was the study's mentor, guiding its development over months of research and drafting. Her perception of the housing problem in general, as well as of the role of housing in economic growth and income distribution and of policy measures to tailor housing to the circumstances of low-income families, helped shape the analytical foundations of the study. She provided the framework of chapter two, most of what is valuable in chapter seven, and insight that improved the rest. John M. Carson designed the comparisons of housing cost and household incomes in chapter five and undertook much of the field work. In meetings and discussions he shared with us his perception of housing conditions and policies in developing countries. Without his enthusiasm and perseverance it is doubtful that the study would have emerged in its present form. Douglas H. Keare originally framed the cost-income comparisons of chapter five and contributed in many other ways to the analytical content of the study. He carefully read all drafts and made many suggestions that improved their structure.

Beyond this circle of principal researchers, special thanks are due to those who helped in a variety of other ways to prepare the study: Pamela Brigg, Monique Cohen, John C. English, George Kottis, Carroll Long, Anna Sant'Anna, and Eleanor Sebastian. Mary Ann Heraud, Anne McKenna, Gwen Ritchie, and Darlene Hines supervised the typing of the manuscript with care and thoroughness. Wing Ning Pang skillfully assisted John Carson in presenting the data in chapter five and with many of the arguments of chapter seven. Nancy Hwang, Lea Adams, and Abdelaziz Khogali provided able research assistance. Michael A. Cohen contributed much to the overall design of the study in its early stages and provided encouragement throughout the writing process. Harrison Wehner later contributed many ideas, especially to chapters three and six.

All those who helped prepare this study are deeply indebted to numerous public officials and scholars in the cities in which field work was undertaken—Ahmedabad, Bogotá, Hong Kong, Madras, Mexico City, and Nairobi—who answered our questions with perception and unfailing good grace. We wish particularly to thank P. B. Buch, N. R. Desai, Jamnadis Patel, Ram Setya, and I. D. Vyar in Ahmedabad; Jorge Bernal, Lauchlin Currie, Victor Flores, Daniel Gonzalez, Fernando Jiménez, Anibal Lopez, and Alberto Vásquez Restrepo in Bogotá; D. J. Dwyer, Donald P. H. Liao, and Benjamin Mock in Hong Kong; M. George, P. K. Nambiar, F. B. Pithavadian, K. Rajaram, and K. R. Ramaswamy in Madras; Ruben Gleason Galicia and Jesus Silva Herzog in Mexico City; and Aveling Abutti, K. J. Ball, A. J. Marshall, Braz Menezes, A. A. Ngotho, J. A. O' Loughlin, Sam Rionge, G. J. Verbeek, and Saad Yahya in Nairobi.

Many other colleagues in the World Bank and elsewhere gave valuable assistance, and it is possible to thank only a few of them here. Shankar Acharya, Anthony Churchill, Harold B. Dunkerley, John R. Harris, Bertrand Renaud, and Herman G. van der Tak made many suggestions that improved the analysis and presentation. In addition, I owe thanks to Kenneth Bohr, Elizabeth Grimes, Callisto Madavo, Richard Metcalf, Alfred P. Van Huyck, and Margaret A. Wilcox for expert help on particular aspects of the study. Special gratitude is due to Ravi Gulhati, director of the Development Economics Department, whose discerning comments on various drafts were an important factor in improving their content. The final manuscript was edited by Goddard W. Winterbottom; the index was prepared by Katharine Tait.

Washington, D.C.   Orville F. Grimes, Jr.
January 1976   Development Policy Staff
                                                      The World Bank

Housing

for Low-Income

Urban Families

One

Introduction and Summary

THE MUD-BRICK, THATCHED-ROOF HOUSES of Africa, the flat-roofed dwellings of the Middle East, and the pitched-roof, stilt-supported structures of Southeast Asia are typical of the variety of housing styles that enrich the human heritage. Behind this diversity, however, housing reflects similarities based on the need for it to serve common purposes of working, eating, sleeping, childrearing, and leisure.

Perceptions of the role of housing have been broadening. In the past, when housing was looked upon primarily as a physical phenomenon, policies for the provision of housing centered on construction costs, combinations of alternative material inputs, and the level of standards and finish. In recent years, however, the economic and social costs and benefits of housing have begun to receive more emphasis. Housing not only provides shelter for a family but also serves as a center of its total residential environment. As a focus of economic activity, as a symbol of achievement and social acceptance, and as an element of urban growth and income distribution, housing fulfills a social need and satisfies criteria for remunerative urban investment.

This study is intended to contribute to the discussions of housing policy options among urban planners and policymakers in developing countries. It does not attempt to analyze the optimal allocation of investment in urban areas or to suggest what place housing should have in such investment. There is no argument for a shift of capital and other resources from other sectors into housing. Instead, the principal intention is to achieve a better understanding of the workings of the

3

urban housing market, especially as it affects low-income families, so as to bring about an improved use of the resources already used for housing and to allow new resources, which would otherwise lie idle, to be used effectively to improve the housing of the poor.

Housing and urban growth

The considerable importance of housing to the urban and national economy contrasts sharply with housing conditions and official policies that exist in many developing countries. For all but the middle- and upper-income groups, housing is usually costly in relation to income and the quality of dwellings available. Cramped, crowded, and unsanitary settlements are the lot of low-income families, conditions that debilitate their energy and reduce national productivity. Families in illegal *favelas, tugurios,* or *bidonvilles* constantly face the threat of eviction as well as scarcities of water, sewerage, and transport. Often, under the banner of slum clearance, low-income groups are removed to higher-quality dwellings located far from income-earning opportunities and asked to pay rents they cannot afford.

As the movement of population to urban areas accelerates, the social costs of haphazard growth are certain to rise. As shown in Table 1.1, by 1980 nearly one-third of the people in developing countries—some 995 million—will live in cities.[1] The urban populations of Asia and Latin America will have more than doubled, and that of Africa will have nearly tripled. By the year 2000 more than 2,000 million people, about 44 percent of the population of the developing world, are likely to be living in cities.

As in the past, a portion of these new urban residents will undoubtedly come to the cities to escape conditions of temporary insecurity in the countryside. This kind of migration occurred in West Malaysia from 1948 to 1960, swelling the squatter populations of Kuala Lumpur and other cities; in South Asia, when millions moved to Calcutta,

1. This figure is based on preliminary U.N. statistics, using the conception of "urban population" as it is defined by each nation. Since many countries include all localities of more than 3,000 to 5,000 people as urban, whereas others use a much higher cutoff, these data are not strictly comparable across countries. The latest U.N. statistics, based on a standard definition of "urban" as all localities of 20,000 people and over, predict that about 31 percent of the developing world will be urban by the year 2000, compared with 22 percent in 1980 and 15 percent in 1960. See United Nations, *Growth of the World's Urban and Rural Population, 1920–2000* (New York: United Nations, 1969), p. 59.

Table 1.1. Estimated Urban Population of Developing Regions,
1960, 1980, and 2000, and Average Annual Growth Rate, 1960–80
and 1980–2000[a]

Developing region	Estimated urban population (millions of persons)			Average annual growth rate (percent)	
	1960	1980	2000	1960–80	1980–2000
Africa[b]	40	112	289	5.3	4.8
Asia[c]	290	646	1,365	4.1	3.8
Latin America	105	237	464	4.1	3.4
Total	435	995	2,118	4.2	3.8

a. With the conception of "urban" as defined by each nation.
b. Excludes South Africa.
c. Excludes Japan.
Sources: U.N. Statistical Office, *Urban-Rural Projections from 1950–2000* (New York, October 1974).

Karachi, and Hyderabad after the Partition of India and Pakistan in 1947; and in Zaïre in the early 1960s, when some cities grew at annual rates of 20 percent and more. The majority of persons, however, will probably migrate because they perceive an opportunity to earn a higher income and live a better life in the city.

If standards of living are to rise commensurately with these opportunities, the much denser concentration of urban population over the coming decades will require that far greater attention be given to the provision of housing and other urban services. In most developing countries the most prevalent method of urban residential expansion is the formation of squatter settlements—neighborhoods at or beyond the margin of the law because the housing does not meet existing standards of ownership and structural quality. These settlements, especially in African cities, usually grow at low densities, which can often bring about high attendant costs of extending road, water supply, and sewerage networks. Travel to sources of employment becomes more difficult and road congestion increases. Many persons are denied access to income-earning and social opportunities. Population concentrations also increase exposure to pollution, already a serious problem for many cities in developing countries.

This litany of urban problems is all too familiar. A significant part of the problem, however, arises from a misperception of the causes of the "housing crisis" that makes housing conditions in most countries appear worse than they actually are. In a handful of countries that have responded imaginatively to housing problems, solutions are geared to the employment needs and purchasing power of low-income urban families; standards of construction are realistic, so that the poor can afford the housing provided; and the housing is so situated that it gives them access to jobs and social services. But governments more frequently tend to promote unrealistically high standards of housing for the poor, so that default and delinquency in rental payments are common, transport to work is costly, and housing built for the poor is raided by middle-income groups whose demand for housing also remains unsatisfied. Slum demolition and removal make matters worse by destroying existing housing stock. Unrealistically high standards for new dwelling construction and the refusal to accept existing low-quality dwellings as even an interim solution make it all the more difficult to meet the investment needs of rapid urban population growth.

Although inappropriate housing standards form the principal barrier, other imperfections also contribute to widening the gap between housing demand and supply for the urban poor. Where they are effective, zoning and building code restrictions tend to inhibit mixed land uses and thereby restrict the growth of housing adjacent to employment centers. Housing finance institutions typically are embryonic, and the limited resources available often go first to middle- or upper-income groups, at interest rates representing explicit or implicit subsidies. Other scarce resources are also used to provide high-cost subsidized housing to a small fraction of the population. These policies have in common a piecemeal approach to housing problems rather than a concerted effort in which housing, land use regulations, public services, the transport network, and employment are treated in concert.

Measures of the severity of the housing problem

Past approaches to housing have generally taken the form of calculating a present and future housing "deficit" relative to housing "needs." These "needs" were not related to the availability of resources; the implicit or explicit conclusion of such calculations was that to commit resources to urban housing, particularly for low-income groups, was to squander such resources in a bottomless pit.

Deficit estimates suffer from two important drawbacks. First, problems of definition make their use on a comparative basis hazardous and at best confusing. The housing stock, for example, may be represented by the number of dwelling units, by total cost of construction, or by floor space. Measures of residential density include dwellings per unit of land area, persons or households per room or per dwelling, and the proportion of land occupied by buildings. Perhaps most important, physical yardsticks do not begin to measure the variations in the quality of dwellings located sometimes within a few hundred feet of one another. Neighborhood noise, nearness to paved streets, frequency of refuse collection, and other aspects of the environmental quality of housing have yet to be combined in standard measures of "housing quality" that will permit comparisons across countries.[2]

Second, measures of deficit that rely on data for slum and squatter housing as proxies for inappropriate housing tend to overstate the seriousness of the housing problem (see Table A1 in the statistical appendix). Although such housing may be illegal or may be built from traditional materials, it is not necessarily of an unacceptably low standard. In most cities much of this housing provides both adequate shelter and good access to employment. Some of it is quite substantial. To condemn all dwellings below an arbitrary standard is to complicate the task of providing a minimum of shelter to all urban families and to render the housing problem larger than it need be.

Scope and conclusions

The study is introduced by a survey of housing conditions in developing countries. Four factors dominate the housing situation in most cities: income (the most important), city size, rate of urban population growth, and the policy context of housing provision. Together, these elements produce a wide diversity in the options open to developing countries in treating their housing problems. Even in high-income countries, some of which have mounted impressive housing programs without large subsidies, many of the urban poor are relegated to squatter areas remote from jobs or social services. Middle-income countries, with more limited means, have often successfully stimulated private developers by a variety of policies, including loans for building materials, provision of water, sewerage, and other services, and adoption of realistic building codes. Many encourage self-help building, as in sites-and-services and squatter-upgrading schemes, which are also a feature of the housing programs of many low-income countries. But other governments at all income levels have adopted standards that

2. For further discussion of this point, see Wallace F. Smith, *Housing: The Social and Economic Elements* (Berkeley, Calif.: University of California Press, 1970), pp. 44–48.

inhibit self-help construction and thereby set the price of housing beyond the reach of most low-income families.

When viewed as shelter or living space only, dwellings tend to be built without regard for their environment or the services needed to support them and their inhabitants. Yet the true importance of housing lies in the fact that it is a package of services: land, public facilities, and access to jobs, as well as the structure itself. Through multiplier effects, housing can significantly increase income and employment. Estimates for Korea and Colombia, for example, suggest that housing construction ultimately brings an increase in national income of about twice the original investment. Housing construction is particularly well suited to absorbing low-skilled labor and in this way can provide a foothold in the city for many poor families. By using currently unemployed or underemployed labor, investment in housing can lead to a more efficient use of existing resources.

If housing is to fulfill its potential of conferring a wide range of benefits to individuals and cities, it is essential for design standards to ensure that housing costs are within reach of low-income families. Minimum requirements for lot size, for example, may allow more living space, but the resulting high cost of land may force households farther to the outskirts of the city or rule out purchase altogether. Capital-intensive building techniques may be the result in part of interest subsidies, overvalued exchange rates, and other stimuli in whose absence labor-intensive methods using traditional materials would have been preferred. Fragmented or overlapping responsibilities among city agencies hamper coordination of water, transport, and other public services associated with housing.

Attempts to deal with these problems have often translated the housing "needs" of poor families into a target for investment without adequate appreciation of these cost elements or of how they compare with household incomes. The focus of this study, by contrast, is on housing that low-income families can afford. A study of housing costs and incomes undertaken in six cities—Ahmedabad, Bogotá, Hong Kong, Madras, Mexico City, and Nairobi—provided a basis for analyzing the provision of housing to low-income groups. These cities cannot, of course, be regarded as a comprehensive sample, but they do represent a wide, and at the same time fairly typical, range of housing experience and income levels in developing countries. To provide a broader base for the analysis and conclusions, the information obtained through field work was supplemented whenever possible by the evidence of other research. Furthermore, urban housing cannot be considered in isolation from all housing, including rural; major regional and national policy decisions affect all households regardless of location. Thus, actions of urban developers, consumers of housing, and public authorities that influence housing beyond urban areas are also considered.[3]

The results of the study suggest that the cheapest new housing currently being built is still not affordable by the poor. Under reasonable repayment terms and at an interest rate of 10 percent, one-third to two-thirds of urban families cannot afford the cheapest new housing in the cities studied. Existing housing policies thus exclude not only the poor but also many middle-income families. But under reasonable assumptions about reduced standards and livable space, housing could be brought within the range of all but the poorest families. In Bogotá, for example, a single-family dwelling of 20 square meters, with individual water and sanitation located at the periphery of the city, could be afforded by all but 17 percent of the population—and by all but 14 percent in Mexico City. In some cities row houses and other kinds of housing that economize on land could be afforded in intermediate locations of the city by about the same proportion of families as single-family houses at the periphery. Medium-rise dwellings—up to about five stories—are a viable alternative in many settings. In low-income cities such as Ahmedabad and Madras, however, these measures would still leave about 40 percent of the population unable to afford the cheapest public housing. Other programs, especially sites and services and upgrading of squatter areas, would be needed in these cities to reach the poorest groups.

Policies in countries that are dealing successfully with their housing problems concentrate on reducing unnecessarily high standards and eliminating other imperfections that prevent the housing market from functioning smoothly. Hong Kong and Singapore, among other developing areas, have skillfully combined policy instruments to meet the demand of all but the poorest families and to improve the spatial relation of people and jobs. Standards in Hong Kong's early public housing projects were geared to what was affordable; living units could be expanded by tearing out walls as family incomes grew. Small-scale industries were encouraged to locate in the midst of housing settlements.

Although solutions must be fashioned from the characteristics and the unique needs of each city and nation, enough ingredients of success are known to provide guidance for improved housing policy.

3. Provision of housing in rural areas as such is best handled in the context of rural development. It is therefore not specifically covered in this study.

Two

The Urban Housing Situation in Developing Countries

MOST CITY DWELLERS find some form of housing, ranging from the spacious dwellings of the rich to the hovels in which the poor, in their attempt to earn a living, are beset by hunger, illness, and the elements. Housing is as varied and complex as the societies it serves, but certain constant features—income, city size, rate of urban growth, and policy—dominate and shape the housing situation in any given city.

Income is the most important element in shaping the housing situation. On a nationwide scale income determines a country's capacity for housing its population at standards that will not distort allocations between urban and rural investment. Per capita income and its distribution among households, along with the price of housing, establish the amount of housing that particular families can afford. A country with a relatively high per capita income but in which the income is heavily concentrated among upper-income groups may still have a difficult housing problem. A country or city with a better income distribution will find it easier to devise policies to solve its housing problems. The distribution of income also has a spatial dimension: there are relatively rich cities in low-income countries, and relatively poor cities in high-income countries.

City size, a second major element, affects accessibility to employment, commercial and social services, and other urban facilities. The value of accessibility is reflected in land prices, which vary greatly among different types of cities. In large, relatively old cities, land with

10

ready access to urban facilities is generally scarce and therefore high priced. This scarcity is aggravated when large quantities of public and private land are not used with the intensity required of a central location. Land is cheaper on the outskirts of such large cities, but often this is because provision of water and other services has failed to keep pace with urban expansion, with the result that such outlying areas are not integrated with the other parts of the city. Infrastructure is often poor, and inadequate urban transport makes access to employment and urban facilities costly and time consuming. In contrast, in provincial centers and other smaller cities even centrally located land may be low in price. Characteristics of a national urban system—the number of principal cities and their size—thus affect the housing situation in a country.

The rate of urban growth is a third important element in the housing situation and one that intensifies the problems created by size. Many cities in developing countries have grown faster in the last twenty-five years than at any previous time in their history. In most of these cities urban planning and infrastructure (roads, water supply, sewerage, electricity, schools, health clinics, and the like) have lagged behind city growth. Vast areas of unserviced urban sprawl are often the result. Public transport has usually failed to keep pace with urban growth and thereby created pressure for private ownership of motor vehicles, with resulting traffic congestion.

Beyond these elements, wide variation exists in housing conditions among cities with similar income, size, and growth rates, and it is here that the impact of differing policies and policy administration is also felt. Not only the resource potential but also the manner in which these resources are mobilized and applied are critical for the housing situation.

Topography and climate are modifying rather than determining factors. Hilly and marshy land, a site surrounded by mountains or the sea, and sites susceptible to earthquakes are all relatively difficult to develop. But although topography has aggravated poor housing conditions in some countries, many cities have been able to turn their physical settings into an advantage. The filling of marsh and seashore has often created publicly owned land in central locations, and rivers and lagoons have been used to create "lungs" for otherwise densely settled areas.

It would be hazardous to ascribe general weights to the various factors determining housing conditions, because the housing situation in each country and city represents a unique combination of influences from income, size, rate of growth, topography, and policy and administration. Interactions among these components are as critical to the outcome as their individual weights.

Analysis is further complicated by the absence of even reasonably accurate data. Pitfalls related to attempts at defining "urban" populations, with the associated difficulties of intercity and intercountry urban data comparisons, have been covered widely in many other studies.[1] The limitations of data on "substandard," "slum," and "squatter" housing, however, are less well known. With the exception of a handful of cities that have been particularly active in improving housing, it is consequently not possible to estimate actual changes in urban housing conditions over the past several years. Even more important, terms such as "slum" and "squatter" are pejorative rather than descriptive. Typically, estimates of "substandard" housing include much housing of relatively high quality that may lack legal tenure, services, or both. Many existing estimates are useful as broad reckonings of housing performance but may be misleading for purposes of economic analysis. Thus, data of this kind must be used with great caution and supplemented with other evidence whenever possible.[2]

Given these caveats, income clearly is the principal determinant both of a country's present housing conditions and of its capacity for improving housing. The cities of the Sahel in Africa and of South Asia are not able to afford the relatively high-standard, high-cost housing solutions shown to be feasible in Singapore—or even some of the measures taken by middle-income countries—without causing an undue drain on public resources from other sectors. Developing countries, like others, exhibit an income continuum, but a rough division into those with relatively high income (per capita income of more than US$450 a year), medium income (per capita income of from US$150 to US$450 a year), and low income (per capita income of less than US$150 a year) forms a useful organizing framework for a consideration of housing conditions.

1. These issues are discussed, for example, in Eduardo E. Arriaga, "A New Approach to the Measurement of Urbanization," *Economic Development and Cultural Change*, vol. 18 (January 1970), pp. 206–18; Gerald S. Goldstein and Leon N. Moses, "A Survey of Urban Economics," *Journal of Economic Literature*, vol. 11 (June 1973), pp. 471–515; and Roy W. Bahl and Elliott R. Morss, "The Urban Lending Program of the IBRD: The Case for Comparative Urban Information," Urban and Regional Report no. 75-3 (Development Economics Department, World Bank, 1975; processed).

2. Specifically, estimates of housing deficit or needs were found to be so misleading that they could not be used. See Table A1, note f., in the statistical appendix.

Relatively high-income developing countries

Many of the relatively high-income developing countries have long-established principal cities such as Beirut, Caracas, Hong Kong, Mexico City, Santiago, and Singapore. These cities, although differing among themselves, share common characteristics when compared with cities in poorer countries. Some have tended to grow more slowly in the 1960s than cities in middle- or low-income countries because their main spurt of growth was already behind them.

Comparative performance of the housing market

There are, however, important differences among the countries and cities in this category. Some, notably Singapore and Hong Kong, have created conditions in which the bulk of the population is housed in serviced dwellings with good access to income-earning opportunities and urban facilities. Well-conceived and executed policies in these cities have included the development and control of serviced land and urban transport, the encouragement of vigorous, competitive construction and construction-materials industries, and the provision of long-term credit for housing. Private developers have thus been able to provide about 45 percent of housing requirements in each city. Impressive housing construction programs that have been tailored to dwelling standards affordable by low-income groups have differed considerably between the two cities, as well as within each city through time. Yet these programs currently meet about 40 percent of the housing requirements without large subsidies. Only about 15 percent of the population still lives in slums and shacks, but public housing programs are expected to accommodate these families by the end of the 1970s.

Several other countries in this income category have taken steps to facilitate the working of the housing market in such a way that the private sector has been able to make a substantial contribution to providing housing for upper- and middle-income groups. Beirut and Santiago have undertaken major land development programs and attempted to make housing finance available. Manufacturers and other employers have sometimes played a substantial role by guaranteeing their employees' housing loans. The availability of housing is a frequent fringe benefit of employment in the public service. In Jamaica the government that took office in mid-1972 realized that existing public programs, which included public sale and rental dwellings and a small amount of self-built housing and cooperatives, were inadequate for existing low-income populations. Consequently, land-servicing schemes were adopted that used a maximum of self-help in construction as a way of tackling the proliferating squatter problem. These programs are scheduled to account for a large share of housing expenditure over the coming years.

It is striking, however, that in some of these countries up to 50 percent of the population is forced to live in slums or unserviced squatter areas, usually without security of tenure (see Table A1 in the statistical appendix). These data should be interpreted with great caution, however, since they may overstate the severity of the housing problem. Many of these families are in middle-income groups with an established capacity to earn steady incomes and save. In the slums of relatively high-income Latin American countries it is not unusual to see refrigerators and television sets connected to pirated electricity obtained from power distribution lines. Existing land, public utility, and financial policies—or the absence of such policies—place serviced land, reasonable housing, and security of tenure out of the reach of such middle-income families. The poor are crowded into the most unsanitary and often the most remote of such squatter areas.

The squatter settlement situation is aggravated by the cycle of demolition and redevelopment occurring as squatter areas—particularly those close to employment centers within the city—become valuable as locations for development of commercial buildings or high-income housing. Relatively high-income countries in particular often tend to overlook the need to legalize and improve low-quality housing as one step toward its eventual transformation to acceptable standards. Instead, by making land acquisition procedures costly and by using prohibitively high standards for construction and the ubiquitous bulldozer, these countries often destroy the existing housing stock and force families to relocate to equally insecure conditions, usually even farther from employment opportunities.

Poor families are the least able to defend themselves against such measures. The social costs of this cycle of demolition are also high. The destruction of fixed capital assets has social dimensions, and the reduction in income of the urban households involved curtails their purchasing power. Relocation of families to sites on the urban periphery may permit alternative forms of economic growth—but at a high social cost that is rarely included in calculating rates of return.

As valuable capital assets are destroyed in this cycle of demolition and redevelopment, restraints on private sector initiative in housing may worsen the problem. In Uruguay, rent control, by discouraging maintenance and new construction, has contributed to a general malaise in housing since its inception in 1943. Although a tripling of rents was authorized in 1967, rent increases have consistently lagged behind the movement of overall prices.[3] Some rents have not even brought in enough to pay taxes on the dwelling.

Mexico City: an illustration

In many ways Mexico City has also exemplified these policies. It is a very large metropolitan area that has been growing quite rapidly, especially in recent years. It is favorably situated on a plateau and enjoys relatively high per capita levels of income. Rent control in the center of the city has distorted the rental market to the point at which rents for identical apartments can vary by as much as 1,000 percent within the same building. Urban renewal and prohibitive building codes have intensified the problem caused by rents, reducing housing availability in the city center and causing tremendous growth at the periphery. Whereas the average annual population increase for the metropolitan area as a whole was 3.5 percent between 1960 and 1970, surrounding districts had annual growth rates as high as 16 to 35 percent.

The city's outward growth has included the movement of high-income groups to enclaves, in which housing prices are high, beyond the southwestern suburbs. Some middle-income groups, in their search for access to the city center, have succeeded in climbing the city's rent gradients, but the cost of their housing is relatively high and is generally of poor quality. The majority in the low-income groups have been forced to locations with poor access to employment and services. They pay relatively small shares of their incomes for housing by squatting. Utilities are usually not available, though there is some pirating of electric power. A high proportion of income and time is spent, of course, on transport to employment.

One such area is Netzahualcoyotl, with a population of more than 1 million. It is located on a dry salt-lake bed, which permits no cultivation. Here the inhabitants face frequent flooding, typhoid in the wet season, and bronchial pneumonia in the dusty dry season. Infant mortality is four times higher in this area than in three low-income areas of Mexico City, and half of that mortality is attributed to bronchial pneumonia and the dusty conditions.[4]

3. A brief synopsis of past housing problems in Uruguay may be found in Thomas E. Weil and others, *Area Handbook for Uruguay* (Washington, D.C.: U.S. Government Printing Office, 1971).

4. David J. Fox, "Patterns of Morbidity and Mortality in Mexico City," *Geographical Review*, vol. 62 (April 1972), pp. 151–85.

In smaller Mexican cities the problems generally appear to be less acute, primarily because distances between employment and housing are shorter. Nonetheless, population growth rates, topographical constraints, and the quality of city government produce a wide variation in housing conditions.

Middle-income developing countries

Developing countries in the middle-income range account for some 30 percent of the urban population of developing countries; they also have some of the largest cities and clearly have a housing problem of major proportions. In some cases up to 80 percent and even 90 percent of the population is housed in "slums and unserviced squatter settlements" (see Tables A1 and A2 in the statistical appendix). These data may exaggerate the severity of the housing problem. The extreme diversity of these countries must also be emphasized. Countries are included from sub-Saharan Africa, Asia, the Middle East, North Africa, Europe, and Latin America. Their cities tended to grow very rapidly in the 1960s. The African countries in particular have high rates of urban growth and large proportions of shack dwellers in their principal cities. The older cities of the countries bordering the Mediterranean are larger, but they have slower rates of urban growth, and their inner-city slums often form the hard core of the housing problem. The Asian and Latin American countries fall between these extremes and vary significantly in the number of cities in each country and in city size.

It is important to note that some middle-income countries—and particularly some of the cities in this group—have also succeeded in creating an environment in which the private sector has been able to meet the needs of all but the poorest sections of the community. One example is São Paulo, a relatively high-income city with a population of some 8 million. Only 20 percent of the households have an annual income below US$1,500.[5] The bulk of the population has been housed through the operation of the private market, with employers making a contribution, principally through financial guarantees. There are access problems, but in comparison with other cities of similar size they are not severe, and efforts are being made to meet them.

5. Adolfo Figueroa and Richard Weisskoff, "Viewing Social Pyramids: Income Distribution in Latin America" (paper presented at ECIEL Conference on Consumption, Income and Prices, Hamburg, Federal Republic of Germany, October 1–3, 1973).

Housing initiatives on limited resources

Vitality of the private sector is not limited to high-income cities. Squatter settlements often provide examples of enterprise and initiative that reflect the amounts families can spend on housing and public services. Newly arrived migrants are often aided in finding affordable housing at suitable locations by squatter residents who came earlier from the same village. In Ankara, Turkey, this occurs much more frequently in squatter (*gecekondu*) housing than in other areas of the city.[6] In the People's Republic of the Congo large-scale public programs in Brazzaville have been absent, but so has slum demolition. For the most part, low-income residents have been left to their own devices. The results, considering the low incomes of squatter residents and topographical limits on building, are by no means negative.[7] Building materials and maintenance reflect the capacity of the families to pay. Streets and pathways constructed by the squatters have stood up well through time. In New-Bell, a densely populated district of Douala, Cameroon, streets and paths are generally well maintained despite the inadequacy of other public facilities such as water, sewerage, and drainage.

Middle-income countries clearly have limited resources for the provision of housing for low-income groups. The most fruitful policies therefore have usually been directed toward encouraging self-help in an environment of secure land tenure, flexible building codes, credit through building materials loans, and provision of public utilities and social services. Several middle-income countries have sought to stimulate housing by increasing the supply of its components—land, utilities, and public transport—although not actually constructing dwelling units. Extension areas are surveyed and layouts are established before occupation. Water pipes are laid in anticipation of squatter settlements. These efforts reduce the costs of assembling the components of housing for individual poor families and often they are accompanied by public commitments for transport linking the newly developed land to services and employment.

In Malaysia, in an entirely different situation, the private market also operates well. The six largest Malaysian cities are all of medium size with populations ranging from 100,000 to 700,000. Incomes are relatively high. Only 8 percent of the households in these cities have in-

6. See Iris Kapil and Hasan Gencaga, "Urbanization and Modernization in Turkey," Discussion Paper no. 10 (Ankara, Turkey: U.S. Agency for International Development, July 1972; processed).

7. See P. Haeringer, "L'Urbanisation de masse en question" (Abidjan: Office de la Recherche Scientifique et Technique Outre-Mer, 1970).

comes of less than US$400 a year, as shown below, and nearly 50 percent of households have incomes over US$1,200 a year.[8]

Household income (U.S. dollars)	Households	
	Percent	Cumulative percentage
0–400	8	8
400–600	11	19
600–1,200	33	52
1,200–1,600	13	65
1,600–1,999	27	92
Over 2,000	8	100

Government land preparation and intervention in the land market have helped to make land available at relatively low prices. The small size of the cities, together with efficient bus services, has meant that access is not a serious problem. Malaysian financial institutions are highly developed, and there are vigorous and competitive building construction and construction materials industries. Through loan guarantees, employers have helped their employees to purchase housing. The typical housing style is a one- or two-story row house, which is economical of land and land development cost and particularly well suited to running a small business on the premises.

Upgrading squatter settlements

The sites-and-services approach, which services urban land and makes it available in small plots so individual households may build their own dwellings, is particularly suited to countries in which neither the financial nor the administrative resources are available for constructing public housing or in which it is not appropriate to use them. In these programs land plots are leveled and furnished with access roads, drainage, water, sewerage, and electricity. Schools, health clinics, refuse collection, fire protection, and other services may also be provided. Dwellings and community structures are built largely by the project participants, who may also help in road formation and the laying of water and sewer pipes. Efforts are usually made to increase jobs in the project area—for example, through encouraging small-scale industries—and increasing attention is paid to locating

8. The six cities are Kuala Lumpur (700,000), Georgetown (350,000), Ipoh (260,000), Johore Bharu (150,000), Klang (100,000), and Malacca (100,000). Adapted from Kingsley Davis, *World Urbanization 1950–1970*, vol. 1 (Berkeley, Calif.: Institute of International Studies, University of California, 1969). Income statistics are derived from World Bank data, as supplied by the government.

projects within reach of major markets and centers of employment. Financial arrangements vary widely. Costs of water and other utilities are recovered through user charges or included in project rental payments. Because schools, markets, and other facilities benefit the city as a whole, their costs typically are met from municipal revenues rather than from rental payments of project participants. Moreover, social costs may indicate the need for explicit or implicit subsidies in the use of land in central locations, in which families cannot afford to pay full market value.

Sites-and-services programs are often complementary to efforts to upgrade existing squatter areas. The objective in such upgrading is to avoid, insofar as possible, the dislocation of residents when roads and public facilities are introduced. In the low-density settlements of most African cities and at the outskirts of most other cities this objective can usually be achieved, but most central city slums and squatter areas of long standing are so densely populated that services cannot be introduced without removing a few structures. Even when removal is held to a minimum, some families may have to be rehoused.

The evolution of housing policy in Zambia illustrates the application of sites-and-services and squatter-upgrading programs to the needs of low-income households. Before independence was achieved in 1964, housing policy was heavily influenced by the needs of the mining industry. Filling the housing requirements of salaried mine workers left few resources for housing the self-employed or unemployed. As in other African cities, housing was built for single occupants: men who worked a short time in the mines while their families remained in the villages. As economic conditions improved and entire families migrated, such housing became ill suited to the demands of the larger households.[9] In Kabwe and Kitwe the landholdings and operations of the mining companies further distorted the overall availability of land for residential settlement, but in Luanshya, a mining town in which fewer such distortions existed, the housing problem was markedly less severe.

Limited national resources drew the attention of Zambian policymakers to serviced plots, since public funds were not available to build complete houses for each family. A major effort has been made in Lusaka, Chingola, and (especially) Ndola; in the last city completed dwellings on sites-and-services plots accounted for nearly 10 percent of the housing stock in 1973 (see Table 2.1).

9. In India, however, many urban dwellings still serve men who send small remittances to their families in rural areas. Calcutta contained over 1 million "single-member households" in 1961, according to the census of that year.

*Table 2.1. Sites-and-Services Plots Completed and Planned,
Zambia, 1973*

| City | Estimated population (thousands) | Estimated housing stock (thousands) | Sites-and-services plots occupied | | Sites planned[a] |
			Number	Percent of total housing	
Chingola	194	33.2	985	3.0	2,830
Kabwe	111	19.8	280	1.4	1,680
Kitwe	311	52.4	812	1.5	6,200
Livingstone	54	11.0	149	1.4	1,530
Luanshya	113	19.4	215	1.1	1,780
Lusaka	381	73.2[b]	4,619	6.3	12,100
Mufulira	130	20.8	225	1.1	2,280
Ndola	220	39.9	3,850	9.6	5,700

a. Second National Development Plan, 1971–76.
b. Rough estimate.
Source: World Bank data, as supplied by the government.

Zambia has also attempted to upgrade existing squatter areas through the provision of utilities and services to income groups unable to afford sites-and-services plots. Elsewhere in Africa, Dakar is assisting *bidonvilles* through a program that is similar in many respects.

Governments such as those of Zambia, Tanzania, and Senegal have come to view sites-and-services and squatter-upgrading projects more as part of an integrated housing policy than a series of unique projects. As of 1973 sites-and-services projects were a part of the national development plans of at least thirteen countries. By the same year Turkey, Chile, India, Pakistan, and Iraq had each completed more than 50,000 sites-and-services plots, and Operación Sitio in Chile had provided over 200,000 serviced plots in three years.[10] The governments most interested in sites and services and squatter upgrading are often the ones which, having had extensive experience in trying to provide low-cost housing by conventional means, recognize the futility of building public housing to fit every pocketbook.

The squatter-upgrading and sites-and-services methods have had considerable success where they have been carefully implemented and have created a much improved immediate environment and a basis for future development as living standards rise. More countries are

10. "The Popular Building Programme" (Nairobi: National Christian Council of Kenya, 1972). See also W. Grindley and R. Merrill, *Sites and Services: The Experience and Potential* (Washington, D.C.: World Bank, May 1973; processed).

now overcoming the objections that prevented the use of the sites-and-services approach in the past. The principal problems, however, are that unrealistically high building standards still make this approach wasteful of land and that the consequent low-density occupation may lead to urban sprawl.

Peru has been one of the most realistic countries in dealing with this problem. Some 200,000 of the 500,000 dwelling units in Lima are in *pueblos jóvenes,* "new towns" that are in effect squatter settlements organized by *barriadas* associations. Middle-income as well as poor families live in these settlements, and many inhabitants now have de facto security of tenure. The quality of this housing stock is high: 54 percent had brick walls in 1970, compared with 65 percent for Lima as a whole.[11] The creation of the Oficina Nacional de Desarrollo de Pueblos Jóvenes in 1969 accelerated the legalization of land tenure for squatters and increased private investment in housing. This activity has been accompanied by a building code requiring that the dwelling be of sufficient quality to permit construction of at least one additional story. Although other public efforts to increase the supply of housing through apartment or house construction or sites-and-services schemes apparently have failed to reach low-income groups in Peru, the acceptance of the *pueblos jóvenes* has permitted private housing solutions for them.

Unfortunately, in contrast to such progressive policies, many other governments of middle-income countries insist on maintaining building standards that prohibit self-help construction by low-income households. The sentiment "construct big, beautiful, and forever" is not unusual, but the resulting high official standards force low-income groups into squalor. In many countries insistence on high standards has been reflected in an unrealistically large minimum size for residential lots, restrictive building codes, limitations on the use of inexpensive construction materials, the tying of credit to high construction standards, and the modeling of citywide infrastructure networks after those of suburbs in high-income Western countries. Programs such as sites and services are rejected on the grounds that they permit "legalized slums." Some governments that have accepted sites and services have set such high standards for lot sizes that the urban poor are excluded, and only middle- and upper-income groups are assisted.

The housing picture again varies greatly from country to country and among cities in a given country. In Korea, for example, except for

11. Douglas H. Keare and others, "The Lima-Callao Metropolitan Area," Urban and Regional Report no. 72-2 (Washington, D.C.: World Bank, October 1972; processed).

Table 2.2. Housing Shortages by City Size, Korea, 1970

Urban population (thousands)	Shortage[a] (percent)
50–99	33.5
100–199	36.3
200–299	41.8
400–499	43.1
500–599	45.6
600–699	42.1
1,000–1,999	46.3
Over 2,000	45.6

a. Based on one dwelling unit per household. No Korean cities had populations of between 300,000 and 400,000 or between 700,000 and 1,000,000. These figures are intended to illustrate the relation between housing conditions and city size; limitations on their use as deficit measures are touched upon in the text.

Source: *A Survey of the Housing Market in Urban Korea* (Seoul: Institute of Urban Studies and Development, Yonsei University, August 1972), p. 29.

cities of fewer than 200,000 people, housing shortages do not at first sight appear to vary with city size (see Table 2.2). One reason, however, is that the relatively serious housing problem in Seoul has benefited from the program of the Korea Housing Corporation, whose efforts have been largely concentrated in that city. Without this additional construction, Seoul's housing situation would probably be much worse.[12] Certainly Seoul and the other larger cities have more serious access and transport problems, which do not show up in these measures of housing deficit.

In El Salvador the efforts of public agencies have so far made few inroads into the demand for housing by all income groups. The number of public housing units produced during 1962–70 was only about one-quarter the number of households established during this period. Moreover, as shown in Table 2.3, the little public housing that has been produced has gone mainly to middle- and upper-income groups. All publicly financed units and 70 percent of publicly constructed units—in addition to 90 percent of privately built housing—went to middle-or upper-income households. The government is aware of the problem and is working to stimulate housing construction through workers' and businessmen's contributions to a National Housing Fund. The Fundación Salvadoreña de Desarrollo y Vivienda Mínima, a private,

12. A possible explanation for the extreme concentration of activities of the Korea Housing Corporation in Seoul is that low-income populations in secondary and smaller cities are too poor to afford the kinds of housing the corporation constructs.

Table 2.3. Income Groups Served by Housing Construction,
El Salvador, 1962–70

Household classification	Monthly household income (U.S. dollars)	Percentage distribution of dwellings constructed			
		Public[a]	Publicly financed[b]	Private	Total
Marginal	0–40	0	0	0	0
Low	40–100	30	0	10	18
Middle	100–240	50	5	30	36
Upper middle	240–400	10	25	20	17
High	Above 400	10	70	40	29

a. Constructed by Instituto de Vivienda Urbano.
b. Financed by Financiera Nacional de la Vivienda.
Source: "Diagnostico de la Situación Habitacional de la República de El Salvador en 1970: Pronóstico y Proyecto de Formulación de la Politica Nacional Habitacional" (San Salvador: Consejo Nacional de Planificación y Coordinación Económica, Instituto de Colonización Rural, Instituto de Vivenda Urbano, Organization of American States, and the United Nations, August 1971).

nonprofit entity, has had notable success in reaching low-income families through serviced plots and is now expanding its activities.

A survey of Manila in 1968 indicated that more than one-fifth of the population of the metropolitan area were squatters and that one-third lived in squatter areas or slums.[13] Squatter and slum dwellers were scattered throughout the central city, but at that time squatting had not extended in any sizable proportions to the outlying areas of Makati and Pasay. These relatively new middle- and upper-income suburban areas had so far succeeded in keeping squatters out. Thus, squatters were heavily concentrated in Manila City (where they made up 16 percent of the population), Malabon (42 percent), Caloocan City (52 percent), and Mandaluyong (68 percent). Since 1970, however, the government has succeeded in clearing out some of the central squatter settlements. Those families which have been unable to remain in the inner areas have found themselves far from the city center with formidable access problems. The Sapang Palay resettlement project, for example, involved relocating some squatters more than twenty miles from their original homes. Only a handful were offered jobs around their new dwellings, and the predictable result was that 40 percent of the origi-

13. José V. Abueva, Sylvia H. Guerrero, and Elsa P. Jurado, Metro Manila Today and Tomorrow (Final Report 1972, Institute of the Philippine Culture, Quezon City, 1972), pp. 66–67. The definition of metropolitan Manila used here includes Manila, Caloocan City, Pasay, and Quezon City, plus four municipalities of Rizal province. This definition is not the same as that used in Table A1 in the statistical appendix.

nal resettled population had returned, a year and a half later, to squatting closer in.[14] Employment opportunities in the outlying areas are
only now being created, slowly. The success of resettlement has been,
not surprisingly, limited; the net result appears to be an increasing
concentration of low-income groups within a few districts of Manila
and some of the surrounding municipalities.

Many of the squatters are middle-income families. The lack of reasonably priced serviced land and of appropriate financial institutions
has made it impossible for them to acquire housing through private
channels. A commercial venture that offered to sell 500 modest
cement-block houses for US$6,000 at a location some 20 kilometers
(12.4 miles) from the center of Manila had nearly 6,000 bona fide appli-
cants, all with access to credit, on the first day. Applications had to be
closed, and the allocation was made by lot. The project could not be
expanded immediately because more serviced land could not be found
at reasonable prices.

In Davao, the capital of the Philippine island of Mindanao, the proportion of squatters is not unlike that in Manila, but their situation to
date has been less desperate. The population of the city is only about
15 percent that of Manila. The low-income groups are thus still permitted, unofficially, to occupy land reasonably close to the city center.
Unlike Manila squatters, they seldom live in drainage ditches, in
flooded areas, or under bridges. Unfortunately, policy appears to be
changing. Upper-income families are establishing suburban enclaves,
and squatters are beginning to be resettled to distant areas in other
directions. Davao, though not yet large, has a difficult topography and
is growing rapidly. If the trend toward segregated land use is pursued,
the ease of access to employment, which has permitted Davao's rapid
economic development to date, may be destroyed.

Urban population growth in Zaïre, particularly the extremely rapid
population growth of the unsettled 1960s, and topography are important elements in the housing situation. City dwellers must make an un-
certain tradeoff between crowded or hazardous locations for their
homes and long travel distances and times, since the trips often must
be made on foot. Although Kinshasa's topographical situation is less
constraining than in some of the smaller cities, the city's population,
combined with low-density sprawl, creates conditions under which
many workers must spend two to three hours a day walking to and from
work. Lubumbashi, with a population of 318,000 in 1970, lacks major

14. Morris Juppenlatz, "Urban Squatter Resettlement: Sapang Palay"
(Manila: August 1965; processed).

topographical constraints and has a more favorable housing and intraurban transport situation. Bukavu, with a population of 135,000 in 1970, has some housing and access problems that appear to arise principally from severe topographical constraints.

The argument over standards dominates policy discussions in many of the middle-income developing countries. It also often delays policy formation[15] and the provision of urban services to low-income groups. High standards for utilities and land development tend to limit serviced land to upper-income groups. If the services are subsidized, as is frequently the case, their expansion is limited, and the subsidy may accrue to the wealthier households. The cost of water that is carted to squatter areas is often ten or even twenty times that of piped water. Adherence to high construction standards usually limits public intervention to subsidized housing for civil servants. As a result of such processes the poorer sections of the population, who are frequently regarded as marginal by those who resent the presence of squatter areas, are marginalized by policies that deny them access to jobs, public utilities, and social services such as health and education.[16]

The poorest developing countries

Among the poorest countries, Bangladesh, India, Indonesia, and Pakistan are similar in that all have relatively low rates of urban population growth. The size and number of their cities is large, however, and there are so many people to be housed that the problems seem overwhelming. The absolute numbers of squatters and slum dwellers in Calcutta (more than 1,700,000), Jakarta (more than 1,125,000), and Karachi (more than 810,000) are greater than the populations of some countries.[17] The extreme poverty of the poorest of these settlements, the corrugated cardboard building materials, the families crowded into drainage pipes, the lack of water and sanitation, and the overcrowding are well known.

15. It has been noted that few African countries had an urban policy during the 1960s; see United Nations, *International Social Development Review*, no. 1 "Urbanisation: Development Policies and Planning" (New York: United Nations, 1968), p. 39.

16. Janice Perlman, "The Fate of Migrants to Rio's Favelas: The Myth of Marginality" (Ph.D. dissertation, Massachusetts Institute of Technology, 1970; processed).

17. *U.N. World Housing Survey*, Report no. E/C6/129 (New York: United Nations, 1974; processed).

Poverty alone—household and national—makes housing problems particularly difficult to deal with, but often the lack of realistic policies makes the situation worse. Constraints on national resources limit the use of housing policies that would require substantial public resources. Even the limited public resources necessary to begin formulation and implementation of housing policy are generally not available. Typically, an organizational framework capable of dealing with urban planning and housing problems of this magnitude is lacking, and substantial assistance may be required for its creation. But a start has been made in Calcutta, and Bombay, Karachi, and Jakarta are seeking to establish frameworks for planning and policy. The acceptance of squatter settlements as legitimate forms of shelter, and the provision to these settlements of secure land tenure, credit, water, sewerage, electricity, schools, clinics, and other services would greatly benefit their inhabitants and stimulate private construction.

Programs to improve the lot of low-income families depend in part on the physical layout of squatter areas and prevailing institutional arrangements. Housing policy differences between Calcutta and Madras are illustrative. The *bustees* of Calcutta—areas occupied by small, temporary single-story huts—house about one-third of Calcutta's population. "Statutory *bustees*," governed by special regulations, are subject to tax assessments and enjoy a measure of security of tenure. Much of the land is privately owned, but huts are built and owned by middlemen known as *thika*-tenants, who rent the huts to the occupants. Slum clearance has not proved effective because of the limited resources available, the enormous size of the problem, and the relatively high-income threshold for participation in the program. One estimate suggests that three-quarters of Calcutta's families have incomes lower than the stipulated limit for participation in the government-subsidized slum clearance program.[18] Furthermore, *thika*-tenants are strongly opposed to clearance, since it would deprive them of their livelihood. For these reasons interest has shifted to improvement of the existing *bustees*. Pathways and limited open spaces make it possible to upgrade the *bustees* by installing water, lighting, and drainage and replacing service privies with sanitary latrines. The Bustee Improvement Organisation of the Calcutta Metropolitan Development Authority initially surveyed *bustee* clusters and assessed the investment priorities and is now carrying out an improvement program with central government assistance.

18. See Colin Rosser, *Housing for the Lowest Income Groups: The Calcutta Experience* (London: Centre for Urban Studies, 1970).

In the low-income areas of Madras, houses are packed closely together, located principally on public land where squatters pay no rent. Roofs of coconut palm greatly increase the danger of fire. Service installation cannot proceed without destruction of a great many dwellings. Housing policy first concentrated on a sites-and-services method; about 8,500 sites were completed by 1970, but these were found to be too land intensive. At present the emphasis is on slum clearance and, to a much lesser extent, slum improvement. The Slum Clearance Board is carrying out plans to relocate slum dwellers in three- or four-story tenements on the land previously occupied. (Brick construction is suitable up to this number of floors without need for columns or beams.) But the program's objective of providing suitable housing for all low-income families is handicapped by the need for a heavy subsidy to tenants who cannot afford to pay an economic rent.

In contrast to the largest and oldest Indian cities, which are growing relatively slowly, many medium-size urban centers are expanding rapidly. Several—Durgapur, Rourkela, Ranchi, and Ghaziabad—have heavy industry, particularly steel, as their economic base. Others such as Calicut and Vishakhapatnam are port cities, and still others such as Chandigarh and Bhubaneswar serve as state capitals. With an appropriate mixture of infrastructure, housing, and transport planning, these cities still have an opportunity to forestall the vast unhygienic and otherwise uneconomic growth typical of some of the larger cities. Efforts are under way in the national Fifth Plan to attack the problems of city growth on a more comprehensive basis. Smaller urban centers and new towns are to be encouraged to counter the pull of the large metropolitan areas—but there remains a real danger of a rapid growth of inadequate housing.

The most acute need is access to a possibility of employment. People who sleep in the downtown streets of Karachi, Calcutta, and other cities of South Asia often do so not because they cannot find shacks on the periphery, but because they cannot afford the cost in money or time for daily travel to their homes. Many have dwellings on the city outskirts and visit their families once a week. Some higher-density housing solutions are unavoidable in the long run. The scale of the housing problems in these four countries requires particularly careful analysis and policy formulation if housing is to be improved without diverting resources from higher-priority uses.

The sparsely populated, often landlocked, and less urbanized African countries also form a special category. The absolute sizes of even their large cities are quite small—from as low as 70,000 for Niamey, Niger, to 100,000 for Monrovia, Liberia—but their rates of urban population growth are high. This growth has rarely been able to stimulate an adequate governmental response to housing problems. Governments in these countries have limited resources, and most of their attention has naturally been directed toward increasing agricultural production. Public housing programs and policies designed to stimulate private housing investment have been few, a lack that is reflected in the high annual construction requirements in most of the countries of this group. The proportion and size of the population officially designated as living in slums or uncontrolled settlements is high in cities in the smallest and poorest countries (see Table A1 in the statistical appendix). These problems are also reflected in policies that are well intentioned but unsuited to the needs of low-income families. In the Sudan a government-sponsored low-cost housing program ran into early difficulty because designers had failed to provide interior separation of the male and female living areas. Some families wished to construct partitions down the middle of their dwellings, but they were prevented from doing so on the ground that subletting and consequent overcrowding might ensue.[19] Construction planning must also take account of whether low-income families keep chickens or other animals inside the dwellings.[20]

Few of the small, poor countries have yet been able to formulate urban housing policies. Malawi, an exception, is making an effort to tackle its housing problem by stressing sites-and-services programs as the only feasible way to reach low-income groups. The country's urban population probably will more than double during the 1970s. Even with an interest-free loan from the government and some commercial bank loans, the Malawi Housing Corporation will be able to finance the construction of only about 500 units a year—but a sites-and-services program in Blantyre-Limbe and a planned development in Lilongwe have a capacity of 8,500 plots each.

The Tanzanian government is perhaps the most vigorous in this field, having initiated sites-and-services projects in Dar es Salaam in the mid-1960s. Although these projects often had unnecessarily high standards and consequently did not attract many urban residents, more re-

19. Harold D. Nelson and others, *Area Handbook for the Democratic Republic of Sudan* (Washington, D.C.: U.S. Government Printing Office, 1973).

20. A survey of urban areas of the Punjab in Pakistan showed that about 20 percent of all households kept some birds or animals with them. Of those which did, 50 percent provided covered space for them outside the living area, but fully 43 percent kept them in their own living areas. See Sardar M. Akhtar (ed.), *Low Income Housing in Urban Areas* (Lahore: Board of Economic Inquiry, 1972).

cent efforts, with lower standards to meet urban income levels, appear promising. Other initiatives include upgrading existing squatter areas. The Tanzanian emphasis is on the public sector as a catalyst for private initiative. The government's policy of self-reliance in housing, as in other sectors, represents an imaginative response to the lack of capital and trained manpower. It recognizes that, in countries with severely limited resources, most of the housing effort must be generated by the private sector.

Three

Housing in the Economy

HOUSING ENCOMPASSES FAR MORE than living space and shelter. Its nature and value are determined by the services it offers. These services are varied, including neighborhood amenities, access to education and health facilities, and security, in addition to shelter. Their worth depends upon quality considerations such as design, density, building materials and floor space, and on access to employment and other income-earning opportunities, public facilities, community services, and markets. Next to food, housing is the largest component of the household budget, making up, typically, 15 to 25 percent of total expenditure and, in low-income brackets, anywhere from 5 to 40 percent. But housing is a durable good, unlike most consumer goods in several important respects. First, it is a fixed-location asset. In this respect it forms a significant portion of privately held wealth in most developing countries.[1] Its production requires close coordination with transport networks and water supply, sewerage, and community services. It may yield a source of income in rental payments or as a place of business and so can be directly productive to families. And the benefits to society as a whole—the social returns—are often higher than the returns to private investors.

Residential construction makes up as much as 20 to 30 percent of gross fixed domestic capital formation in countries in which emphasis

1. See, for example, V. M. Jakhade and S. L. Shetty, "Distribution of Urban Household Wealth in India," *Economic and Political Weekly*, vol. 9 (May 1974), pp. 727–34.

is given to housing and about 2 to 5 percent of gross domestic product (GDP) in most developing countries (see Tables A1 and A2 in the statistical appendix). The true importance of housing is greater than these data suggest, especially in developing countries, since self-help construction and commercial activity by independent contractors is not reported at all or is greatly undervalued. (Unrecorded investment is substantial even in industrialized countries.) Implicit rents of owner-occupiers tend to be ignored or underestimated, and rents paid to private property owners often go unreported. The value of subsidized housing may be recorded at less than its cost of production.

Public expenditure on housing usually constitutes a small fraction of total public expenditure at the national level, though for Hong Kong and those countries which give high priority to housing construction the proportion is higher (see Table A3 in the statistical appendix). When expenditure on water supply, transport, and on other housing-related items by cities and other levels of government are included, the overall public involvement in housing is larger. Nevertheless, with a few exceptions government outlays for housing have not been substantial.[2]

The limited evidence available suggests that investment in housing tends to rise faster than GDP growth at low income levels but to taper off at high income levels. Not the richest but the second richest tier of countries seems to invest the most in housing.[3] More research needs to be carried out, however, before conclusions can be drawn about which countries make the greatest demand on financial resources for the development of housing.

These relations were investigated by means of regression analysis on such variables as the rate of urbanization, the degree of urban primacy, the severity of the housing problem, and measures of population, income, and magnitudes of housing investment.[4] The clear negative correlation between housing investment and severity of the housing prob-

2. See also Djauhari Sumintardja, "Lower Cost Housing Problems in Indonesia," *Proceedings of the Third International Symposium on Lower Cost Housing Problems*, ed. Oktay Ural (Montreal, May 1974), pp. 690–706.

3. Leo Grebler, "The Role of Housing in Economic Development" (Third World Congress of Architects and Engineers, Tel Aviv, December 1973). See also E. Jay Howenstine, "Appraising the Role of Housing in Economic Development," *International Labour Review*, vol. 74 (January 1957), pp. 21–33. The most complete time series and cross-section study (1955–1964) of housing's share in GDP and economic growth is W. Paul Strassmann, "The Construction Sector in Economic Development," *Scottish Journal of Political Economy*, vol. 17 (November 1970), pp. 391–409.

4. Results of the significant regressions are reported in Table A4 in the statistical appendix.

lem suggests that countries investing in housing have indeed been successful in reducing the magnitude of the problem. This suggests that attempts to improve the housing situation in developing countries are not, as some analyses have implied, hopeless.

Housing and employment

Investment in housing has a significant impact on income and employment through multiplier linkages. First-round effects are the direct increments to income and employment generated by construction activity. Estimates for Colombia suggest that the income multiplier for housing construction is about 2, and that about seven additional jobs are created for every US$10,000 spent on the construction of dwelling units.[5] This rate of employment creation in housing construction was higher than that for manufacturing and close to that for the economy as a whole. In Korea the income multiplier of housing construction is estimated at 2, and about fourteen additional jobs are created for every US$10,000 invested in construction.[6] Similar results have been found for Pakistan, India, and Mexico.[7] For Peru, the income to residents of *pueblos jóvenes* in Lima resulting from expenditure on construction (including but not limited to housing) was substantial relative to other sectors: construction ranked tenth out of thirty-one sectors in the strength of its multiplier effects on the income of residents of the *pueblos jóvenes*.[8] In industrialized nations the labor used in construction per unit of value added varies from about equal to that in manufacturing to some 60 percent greater. For some developing nations the labor content of housing construction is higher still.[9]

5. Colombia, National Planning Office, *Aspectos Cuantitativos del Plan de Desarrollo* (Bogotá, 1972).

6. Calculated from data for 1968 and 1969, as provided by the Bank of Korea.

7. A. P. Van Huyck, "Preparing a National Housing Policy," manuscript prepared for Office of Housing, U.S. AID, 1974; B. Natarajan, *Economics of Housing in National Development* (Madras: Institute for Techno-Economic Studies, 1972); and W. Paul Strassmann, "Measuring the Employment Effects of Housing Policies in Developing Countries," *Economic Development and Cultural Change* (forthcoming).

8. R. A. Lewis, "Employment, Income and the Growth of the Barriadas in Lima, Peru," Dissertation Series no. 46 (Ithaca, N.Y.: Cornell University, 1973), p. 295.

9. United Nations Industrial Development Organisation, "Construction Industry," monograph no. 2 (Vienna: UNIDO, 1969). See also S. P. Shah and W. Schramli, "Prefabricated Construction in Industrially Developing Countries," *Proceedings of the Third International Symposium on Lower-Cost Housing Problems*, ed. Oktay Ural (Montreal, May 1974), pp. 779–97.

The direct and indirect employment effects of various types of housing construction are not clear. For each dwelling considered separately, the total labor input is generally higher for luxury housing than for low-income housing because of the need for a variety of labor skills, as well as greater size.[10] Yet when all effects, indirect and direct, are considered, as studies of single family dwellings in Colombia, Mexico, and Venezuela suggest, the employment-generating capacity of housing investment by low-income households may in some circumstances be greater than similar spending by high-income households. For example, in these countries about five man-years of work would have been generated with US$12,000 of annual subsidy given to families earning less than US$2,000 a year during 1969–71. If the same amount had been given to families earning more than US$7,000, only two man-years of work would have been created.[11] Another study of the Mexican housing industry showed a slightly higher employment-generation effect for minimum-cost single-family dwellings than for luxury single-family or multifamily structures.[12] Assessment of the employment effects of housing for different income groups is extremely complicated, however; definitions of "minimum" housing may vary. The ultimate incidence of indirect effects, particularly the reinforcing or offsetting effects on savings and consumption in other sectors, is little known.

Other employment benefits are less tangible though not less real. Investment in housing is particularly well suited to absorbing labor resources whose alternative marginal product is low. Newly arrived rural migrants often work for a few years in construction, which provides a springboard to other income-earning opportunities in the city. Construction of low-income housing in stages allows labor to be used gradually, in line with availability. Countries adopting a wide range of self-help, mutual-help, and hired-labor methods have benefited from this flexibility, within which houses can be built at night and on weekends. In high-income countries and for medium-income housing there is a tendency for parts of the work to be subcontracted. If, in addition, labor is mobile and there is less than full employment, an investment program in low-income housing can bring significant amounts of unused or underused labor into production. Housing construction in developing countries can also be used as an anticyclical policy instru-

10. Strassmann, "Measuring the Employment Effects."

11. W. Paul Strassmann, "Empleo en la Construcción, Valor de la Tierra y Financiamiento," *Demografía y Economía*, vol. 7 (1973), pp. 338–49.

12. C. Araud, G. Boon, V. Urquidi, and W. P. Strassmann, *Studies on Employment in the Mexican Housing Industry* (Paris: Organization for Economic Cooperation and Development, 1973).

ment to take up slack in investment and employment. Housing programs consequently should be introduced during a cyclical trough and eased off during a boom period. Unfortunately, some countries have introduced housing programs during cyclical upswings. Whatever the benefits may be, such a step has in many instances contributed to inflationary trends.

Housing and city design

The rapid urbanization of the developing world is increasing the importance of the economic returns from appropriately designed and located housing and urban development. Investment in housing can have a beneficial impact on the spatial layout of urban areas: well-planned housing economizes on the use of urban space and can reduce the cost of providing urban infrastructure. Better location of dwellings in relation to jobs can lessen traffic congestion and increase household take-home pay by reducing commuting expenses. Staged urban development—including coordinated investment in infrastructure, transport, industrial estates, and housing—offers an opportunity for increasing economic efficiency, as is being recognized in many developing countries.

Labor productivity

Another important benefit not captured directly in housing transactions but that represents cost savings both to individuals and to the public is improved health. In a study of relocated miners in Hambaik, Korea, it was found that the health benefits of improved housing could be measured in terms of a yearly saving of fifty clinical visits per hundred of the rehoused population.[13] This translated into annual cost savings of

13. Leland S. Burns and B. Khing Tjioe, "Housing and Human Resource Development," International Housing Productivity Study, University of California, Los Angeles, 1968. See also M. Allen Pond, "The Influence of Housing on Health," Marriage and Family Living, vol. 19 (May 1957), pp. 154–59; Uses of Epidemiology in Housing Programmes and in Planning Human Settlements, WHO Expert Committee on Housing and Health, Technical Report no. 544 (1974); "The Physiological Basis of Health Standards of Dwellings," WHO Public Health Paper no. 33 (1968); Appraisal of the Hygienic Quality of Housing and its Environment," WHO Technical Report no. 353 (1967); and Daniel M. Wilmer, Rosabelle Price Walkley, Thomas C. Pinkerton, and Matthew Tayback, The Housing Environment and Family Life (Baltimore: Johns Hopkins Press, 1962).

$13.94 for each household. This study is one of the few to link improvements in housing with better health in a cost-benefit framework, although the literature abounds with evidence about the association between bad housing and ill health and on the effects of overcrowding on mental health and family life. Other indirect benefits of improved housing include fewer fires—a chronic problem in squatter settlements in Hong Kong, Singapore, and elsewhere before housing programs had substantial impact—and reduced crime.

Such benefits are reflected in higher productivity of better-housed workers. The study of Korea found that average weekly output per worker increased 28 percent, from US$13.00 before rehousing to US$17.40 after rehousing.[14] Similar positive impacts have been noted for cities in Mexico, Venezuela, and Kenya.[15]

Perhaps the most notable way in which housing investment contributes to increases in productivity is by drawing on labor and other factors of production currently unemployed or underemployed and having a relatively high elasticity of supply. Investment in the housing sector, and particularly in low-income housing, should thus not necessarily imply a shift of resources out of other sectors, but a more efficient use of existing resources and the use of resources that would otherwise remain idle.

Criteria for investment

Arguments suggesting that housing is not a productive outlet for investment fail adequately to appreciate these aspects of housing. It is often alleged, for example, that the capital-output ratio of housing construction is high relative to other sectors. A country should invest first, it is argued, in sectors in which relatively few units of capital are needed to produce a unit of output. In manufacturing the ratio has been estimated at 1.07 units of capital to a unit of output for Korea, and about 4 to 1 for India.[16] As investment in first-priority sectors proceeds, the marginal product of capital in the sector declines and its reciprocal, the capital-output ratio, rises to the point at which investment in

14. Burns and Tjioe, "Housing and Human Resource Development."

15. B. Khing Tjioe and Leland S. Burns, "Housing and Productivity: Causality and Measurement," *American Statistical Association, Proceedings of the Social Statistics Section* (1966), pp. 155–60.

16. Ki Choon Han, "Capital-Output Ratio in Korea—A Trial," *Quarterly Economic Research* (Seoul: Republic of Korea, Economic Planning Board, 1964); Jakhade and Shetty, "Distribution of Urban Household Wealth."

sectors with larger ratios becomes profitable.[17] Housing, with ratios
typically 7 to 1 and sometimes higher, should thus wait until investments directly contributing to the growth of output or foreign exchange earnings have been undertaken—or so the argument goes.[18]

Countries are coming to realize, however, that reliance on the
capital-output ratio as the sole indicator of investment choice can lead
to inappropriate policy decisions. The ratio has shortcomings of measurement and of interpretation. Housing output is usually measured as
rents and interest charges, a dubious procedure because housing is a
flow of benefits from services such as shelter, access, employment, and
income, not all of which are captured in rents. In Charles Frankenhoff's analogy, no economist would measure output in manufacturing
by the rental value of the factory premises—yet this is often done in
measurements of housing output.[19] Moreover, since only the aggregate
amount of investment, not its sectoral composition, is generally considered, capital-output ratios in manufacturing (as one example) may appear to be more favorable than they actually are because investments
in housing, transport, and health, which contribute to a more productive industrial labor force, are not included. It is similarly misleading
to assume that physical capital is the only—or even the main—source
of growth. Entrepreneurship, labor skills, and other inputs make important contributions to output. These factors are neither stable
through time nor independent of one another, so the evaluation of their
contribution is extremely difficult.

Even if human skills were included as capital rather than labor and
other measurement problems were resolved, serious questions of interpretation would remain. Changes in factor prices and in capacity utili-
zation alter the capital-output ratio without any investment having
been undertaken. Thus, low interest rates, cheap imports, and high

---

17. This analysis excludes certain definitional issues, in particular from differences between marginal, incremental, and average capital-output ratios,
which are incidental to the overall direction of the argument.

18. Han, "Capital-Output Ratio in Korea"; and Robert N. Grosse, "The
Structure of Capital," in Wassily Leontief and others, *Studies in the Structure
of the American Economy* (New York: Oxford University Press, 1953).

19. Charles Frankenhoff, "The Economic Role of Housing in a Developing
Economy," *Housing Policy for a Developing Latin Economy* (Rio Piedras, P.R.:
University of Puerto Rico, 1966). See also Paul Streeten, *The Frontiers of
Development Studies* (New York: Wiley, 1972), pp. 71–116; Wallace F. Smith,
Housing: The Social and Economic Elements (Berkeley, Calif.: University of
California Press, 1970); and Leland S. Burns, "Capital-Output Analysis of Hous-
ing Programs for Developing Nations," *Proceedings of the Seventh Annual
Meeting* (Chicago: Industrial Relations Research Association, 1964).

wages—features found to some degree in housing markets in many countries—tend to be associated with high capital-output ratios. Perhaps most important, where market mechanisms function poorly, an investment may be valuable chiefly because it removes bottlenecks and speeds the flow of resources to other sectors of the economy. Investment in housing may involve projects whose capital-output ratios, as conventionally measured, may appear high but yield substantial benefits by mobilizing underused resources, using domestic materials in production, and reducing transport costs and congestion.

Housing also is a basis for income earning for some households. In Bogotá, 20 percent of all households in the *barrios* have some economic activity based in the home, compared with a proportion of 5 to 10 percent for the city as a whole. Such income-earning possibilities therefore seem to be more important for low-income families.[20] More generally, dwellings constructed with the assistance of direct government financing and a land subsidy have often been operated as investment properties. In these instances owners may receive from tenants rents that are substantially greater than their own rental payments.[21]

Effects on macroeconomic performance

Policymakers have often been concerned that investment in housing has a significant balance-of-payments impact both because such investment diverts scarce resources from expanding export-earning or import-substituting industries and because the import content of housing is substantial. Generally, however, housing is not a heavy user of foreign exchange. In Central and South America the most commonly used materials—cement or clay block masonry and sheet roofing—are for the most part produced domestically. In Africa wood products used for housing construction have an overall import content of 35 percent; cement, about 33 percent; quarry materials, 25 percent; and cement products, 14 percent.[22] The ratio of net imports to domestic production

20. Planeación Nacional, *Investigación Socioeconómica de la Zona Oriental de Bogotá,* May 1973.

21. Foundation for Cooperative Housing, 1962. See also John R. Harris, "Some Thoughts on a Housing Policy for Nairobi," Discussion Paper no. 78, Institute for Development Studies (Nairobi: University College, 1969).

22. D. A. Turin, "Housing in Africa: Some Problems and Major Policy Issues," in A. A. Nevitt (ed.), *Economic Problems of Housing* (New York: Macmillan, 1967), pp. 200–14.

for residential construction in Mexico and Korea has been estimated to be at most 0.06 and 0.10, respectively, implying that only 6 to 10 percent of every dollar spent on housing is devoted to purchasing imported materials.[23] For high-income housing, by contrast, the import content can be substantial. In Africa virtually all iron and steel products and electrical fixtures and fittings for housing construction must be imported.[24] In earthquake-prone areas ductile steel frames for reinforcement often must be imported. Building methods using precast components that appear cost saving may actually call for substantial amounts of imported equipment. Countries generally only have to import cement and similar materials while domestic productive capacity is built up. From a long-term perspective, therefore, the production of housing—especially low-income housing—usually poses a small burden on the balance of payments.

The argument that investment in housing is inflationary often confuses association with causality. It is true that, in inflation-prone economies, households try to purchase assets such as housing that tend to rise in value with the price level. Their demand for housing as a hedge against inflation can cause house prices to rise further still. Across the economy, however, the most useful criterion is whether housing or nonhousing investment has the greater impact on product and factor prices. Viewed from this standpoint, the available evidence suggests that housing is not inherently inflationary; if used as a countercyclical measure, it can actually offset inflationary trends. Underused labor can be obtained at the going wage, so effects on wage levels are generally negligible. Although skilled workers, foremen, and others whose talents are scarce may receive large wage increases, especially where unions are strong, the contribution to total dwelling cost is typically small. The most pronounced effects probably stem from short-run bottlenecks in supply and delivery of building materials. Before domestic supply is able to adjust, these shortfalls may have to be made up by higher-cost substitutes or imports. In the long run, construction methods can be employed that are geared to local materials. The quality of housing finishes can also be limited, and comprehensive planning can anticipate probable bottlenecks in supply and work to remove them.

The prospect for better housing does not seem to be a principal reason for rural-to-urban migration. Most conceptual and empirical studies suggest that the greater income-earning opportunities in urban

23. Leland S. Burns, *Housing: Symbol and Shelter,* International Housing Productivity Study (Los Angeles: University of California, Los Angeles, 1970), pp. 134–36.

24. Turin, "Housing in Africa," p. 203.

areas explain such migration far more satisfactorily.[25] Migration, however, is partly responsible for the growing scarcity of housing. Realistic approaches to determining and satisfying the housing needs of this newly urban population deserve more attention than is implied by the neglect, in the cities of most developing countries, of housing relative to other sectors. Housing is neither a leading nor a led sector, but one which is attractive to private investment and confers social and economic benefits on both individuals and cities. Efficient and equitable provision of housing, particularly for low-income families, is thus an important objective for urban policy and one which requires a knowledge of the characteristics of housing cost and supply in relation to the incomes of poor families.

25. See R. A. Lewis, "Employment, Income and the Growth of the Barriadas"; Khalid Shibli, *Housing: Short Range Tactics and Long Range Strategy* (Karachi: Planning Commission, Government of Pakistan, 1965); and Guillermo Geisse, *Notas sobre Renovación Urbana de Poblaciones Populares en Areas Metropolitanas* (Santiago, Chile: Universidad Católica, June 1970).

Four

Supply Factors

HOUSING IS A HETEROGENEOUS GOOD, producing a flow of services to households over time. It consists of a series of components that may be produced in various ways and with different costs, standards, and financing options. None of these aspects of supply operate independently; together they determine the total cost of the dwelling. The result is a wide range of housing types that emphasize the substitutability of one component for another. A rise in the price of a particular component prompts a search for ways to economize on it. When land costs are high, for example, construction becomes denser to reduce land costs per dwelling unit. If cement is scarce, other building materials may be substituted in the production process.

Such direct costs associated with the structure itself are, however, only part of the full cost of housing to the consumer and to the economy as a whole. The location of a dwelling, for example, is as much a part of its essence as its plaster and bricks. A dwelling located far from employment opportunities and social services is actually more expensive than one with better access, because travel expenses must be included in the cost of living at that location. Thus, in a well-functioning market, properties with different access but identical in other respects will command different prices to reflect differences in travel cost. At the same time, the full cost of housing to the consumer, including transport costs, may not reflect the social cost of producing housing at a given location. In journeying to work, each resident may impose additional cost on others in the form of road congestion. Low-density sprawl generally increases the cost of extending sewer lines, street networks, and other public services.[1] Failure to take account of transport costs and other spatial considerations in the design of housing can lead to a less efficient city and costlier housing to the consumer—with particularly harmful effects on poor households.

These considerations make it essential for design standards to ensure that housing costs are not unnecessarily high or supply restricted. Unfortunately, housing standards are typically established by those concerned almost exclusively with physical aspects of the dwelling rather than with wider aspects of the residential environment. Official minimum standards for the placement and construction of dwellings are generally higher than families with low incomes can afford or than they deem essential to satisfy their needs.[2] The opposite may be true of standards for community and social services. These standards may simply be unofficial or, if official, may remain unmet. Since schooling, health care, parks, and other public services or amenities are not generally sold in private market transactions, willingness to pay for them is difficult to ascertain. Standards for these services thus often tend to be lower than the needs of low-income populations.

Although housing standards may be labeled "minimum," they may in many cases be established without direct consideration of cost. They may instead be established to improve overall well-being, usually conceived of relative to health and safety. A certain arbitrariness attaches to these standards, because low-level requirements have not been sufficiently tested and classified under various conditions. Nor are there clear guidelines for ranking the importance of service and structural standards. For example, lack of ventilation, sunlight, drainage, and other amenities may be more important to health than the amount of space per person. In the absence of tested criteria, many developing countries turn to standards derived from the experience of developed countries, which generally have different (usually more severe) climates as well as higher incomes and different patterns of development.

In the absence of a cost approach to minimum standards and rationally tested measures of performance and consumers' preferences, most countries adopt "desirable quality targets" as housing standards. The ensuing discussion of the components of housing supply highlights

1. See Real Estate Research Corporation, *The Costs of Sprawl* (Washington, D.C.: Council on Environmental Quality, U.S. Environmental Protection Agency, and U.S. Department of Housing and Urban Development, 1974).

2. John F. C. Turner and Tomasz Sudra, "Housing Needs and Users' Priorities" (Washington, D.C.: World Bank, 1974; processed).

ways in which these standards, dealing with space, materials, and services, hamper the performance of the housing market and the provision of housing to the poor.

Land

To all urban families, land for housing is essential for access to employment, infrastructure, and social services. To low-income families in particular, a piece of land on which basic facilities are provided is its foothold in the urban community. To the city as a whole, a smoothly functioning land market may improve the spatial relation of residential and employment locations.

Provision of land for housing is complicated by the fact that land has many uses other than for shelter and access. Among productive uses, housing competes for land with industrial, commercial, administrative, and recreational uses. Moreover, in most developing countries a strong preference exists for savings in physical assets, usually land, silver, and gold. These assets are strongly preferred because securities and other investments may be unattractive or nonexistent and because inflation tends to erode the value of savings deposited in financial institutions.[3] Land may be greatly valued for prestige purposes or to provide a sense of family stability and security. Some landowners may hold vacant land off the market in anticipation of larger gains later. This aspect of land hoarding, whether termed speculation or savings, may restrict the supply of land for development and therefore raise land prices.

Land price is a major factor in determining the use of land for housing. Differences in land price basically reflect variations in accessibility to the central business district and other centers of work opportunities. The price of land first falls steeply as distance from the city center increases, then more gradually. At peripheral locations, land price may be low enough for a poor family to purchase or rent a small parcel. In intermediate zones, however, land price may rise to a point at which construction of row housing, multistory buildings, or other high-density units may be economically desirable.

This does not mean that all land at a given distance will be equal in value. Even in cities in which employment is highly centralized, access to secondary employment centers within the metropolitan area seems to be an important determinant of land price. Furthermore, such

3. Mohammed Mohsin, "Institutional Financing of Housing Development in India," *Symposium on Role of Housing in National Economy: Selected Papers and Reports*, Paper no. 35. (New Delhi: National Building Organisation, Government of India, and U.N. Regional Housing Centre, 1969).

amenities as schools, parks, markets, and health centers at each location can raise the price of land substantially. By the same token, undesirable or run-down areas, even near the city center, may have much lower values than their accessibility alone would suggest. Such areas are pejoratively called slums, but they provide opportunities to house the poor with access to jobs.

Market prices of land at three locations—peripheral, intermediate, and central—show a considerable increase toward the center in every city, but there is great variation. The sharpest variation generally occurs in large cities. The price per square meter in Seoul varies from US$2.30 at the periphery to more than US$1,000 at the center. In Abidjan the range is from US$0.40 to US$1,390 (see Table A8 in the statistical appendix). There are, however, exceptions to this higher-price rule: in Madras, for example, the price of land located within the city limits may be as little as three times the price of peripheral land.

It is not surprising that land can make up a high proportion of total dwelling cost. Cost breakdowns for middle- and low-income housing in selected cities—Ahmedabad, Bogotá, Hong Kong, Madras, Mexico City, Nairobi, and Seoul—of developing countries demonstrate that land makes up from 12 to 46 percent of total cost for single-family public housing units and from 2 to 15 percent for multifamily units. Unless they are densely grouped, single-story dwellings are economical only when built on low-cost land.

Well-located and amenity-rich land commands a high price. But accessibility as well as amenity features can be altered, often abruptly, by actions of the public authorities who build and widen thoroughfares, create schools and parks, and install water and sewer lines and electricity. Upon the basic locational and amenity characteristics is thus superimposed a set of public actions—space standards and other regulations as well as public investment—that define the conditions under which land development takes place. Since the rises in land price caused by these actions are socially induced, it is increasingly recognized that governments are justified in recapturing a portion of this "betterment" for social use.[4] Capital gains taxation and public acquisition of plots in advance of need are among the tools used to appropriate increases in land value for public use. Such measures can help make serviced land available at more reasonable prices.

If serviced land is made available at unduly high space standards—which means that more land must be acquired to house the

---

4. Theoretically, governments are justified in capturing the entire socially produced increment, but measurement problems, combined with political opposition, have usually made it impossible to do so.

same number of people—poor families may not benefit adequately from sites-and-services programs. When a family formerly paid twice as much rent for a squatter hut than it now pays for a site with double the space, then by the test of the market that family now lives far above the "minimum acceptable standard." Reasons for the adoption of minimum space standards above the acceptable level are, first, that governments are loath to being accused of building slums; second, that since the public looks ahead to rising standards of living, and since new housing is built to last twenty years or more, standards can be said to reflect expectations; and, third, that there is widespread lack of understanding of the costs imposed by excessively high standards. In practice, of course, such space standards are largely theoretical. Public authorities and developers may provide sites at a prescribed space standard, but the plots are likely to become overoccupied as long as demand outstrips the available supply.

Indigenous and traditional housing forms—an alternative that too often is neglected—in many instances use space-saving designs. Houses may be tightly grouped around a common courtyard. The Swahili house, essentially a series of single rooms under one roof, allows flexible allocation of space to individual or extended families. The longhouse of Malaysia is analogous in design, with semidetached shared kitchens. Even for detached housing, cooking facilities may be shared by several families. These designs are sometimes needlessly forsaken for a modern or Western type of house, with higher space standards and consequently higher cost.

Services

Installation of services in the form of roads, water supply, sewerage, drainage, and other utilities turns raw land into land suitable for housing. The capital cost of complete modern urban services is high, however, especially if the services have to be carried long distances to less accessible land or if topography inhibits installation. Although individuals working in groups can and do build roads, schools, and health centers, the servicing of land is generally undertaken by governments, either directly or through public corporations. These services are spatially fixed and have high fixed costs, but eventually they reach a declining average cost when services are provided in large quantities.[5]

5. For a discussion of these issues in the context of water provision to villages, see Robert J. Saunders and Jeremy J. Warford, *Village Water Supply: Economics and Policy in the Developing World* (Baltimore: Johns Hopkins University Press, 1976).

They create great external economies. They are natural monopolies, and efficiency in a given location is best served if a single organization, rather than many competing firms, supplies the service. Even where private enterprise plays a role, governments can license the entrepreneur and control the prices that may be charged for the services provided.

Variation in the cost of providing services is the result mainly of the topography and size of cities. Both capital and operating costs may rise with the increase in the size of an urban area, decline after a certain urban size has been reached, and then, at some later stage, rise again. The marginal cost of a proposed development may thus depend on the stage of urban growth. Differences between capital and operating costs are also great. Water mains and sewers generally require high capital but low operating costs. As a result of physical factors or policy decisions (the setting and maintenance of environmental standards, for example), the marginal cost of raw water supply or sewage removal may rise while distribution and collection costs are constant or falling. Capital costs in water supply are also affected by the availability of water sources; tapping groundwater sources, as in Lahore, Kinshasa, and Abidjan, is usually much cheaper than dams, pumps, reservoirs, and aqueducts such as are needed to supply Bogotá, Lima, Kuala Lumpur, and other cities. Density of development also has varying effects on both capital and operating costs. A higher density may increase capital costs, as in transport, or lower them, as in water supply. In contrast, density does not seem measurably to affect operating, as against capital, costs for most services.

This picture is further complicated by the need to provide services in coordination with provision of the other parts of the dwelling. Although necessary for sites-and-services and other self-help projects, services installed far in advance of completed dwellings tie up resources and can produce windfall gains to landowners. More typical, perhaps, is the situation in which services lag behind construction rather than precede it, a problem largely the result of fragmented responsibility, inappropriate pricing and financial management policy, and lack of coordination among public service agencies.

Coordination requires the making of political choices at all levels of government. Implementation of services is often undertaken by a local government, which is familiar with the specific features of its city. Because of the meager fiscal resources most cities can draw upon from their citizens, however, financing can rarely be a purely local responsibility. If services are financed from property taxes, as in India, inadequacies in tax collection and administration directly influence the amount and quality of services the cities are able to provide. Schools, commercial centers, and other social services of a public goods nature, the beneficiaries of which are difficult to charge individually, are typically financed from municipal or central government budgets; but water, transport, and other services, the beneficiaries of which can be identified, can be financed through user charges whose rationale is based in part upon the fact that the transformation of raw land with services gives urban land more value. Capital gains taxation and other measures discussed earlier that are designed to capture this increased value for the public have often been blunted by political compromise. As a result, land servicing, even if priced at marginal cost, may contain an element of fiscal subsidy for those upper-income groups benefiting from socially induced capital gains.

The availability of facilities and the level of services provided directly concern the lives of people. Electricity and elevators are convenient but costly. Although essential water and sanitary facilities can be shared, the sketchy evidence that exists suggests that individual water supply and, particularly, private toilets are more highly valued by families than larger rooms or stronger walls.[6] Quality of service is as important as quantity. The choice of level of service must therefore be made to accommodate the preferences and willingness to pay of urban households.

Transport

Urban land resources are fixed and must be used where they are found. Thus, the movement of persons and goods from one point to another always involves a cost. Where the urban poor live is of equal and at times greater importance to them than the conditions under which they live. Accessibility to job opportunities is at least as vital to the casual worker and the underemployed as it is to the regularly employed low-income worker. Many otherwise acceptable housing projects have foundered because they were badly located. More important still is the ability to search for and find employment and other income-earning

6. John S. Western and others, "Housing and Satisfaction with Environment in Singapore," *Journal of the American Institute of Planners*, vol. 40 (May 1974), pp. 201–08; Adepoju G. Onibokun, "Evaluating Consumers' Satisfaction with Housing: An Application of a Systems Approach," *Journal of the American Institute of Planners*, vol. 40 (May 1974), pp. 189–200; James S. Plant, "Family Living Space and Personality Development," in Norman W. Bell and Ezra Vogel (eds.), *The Family* (Glencoe, Ill.: Free Press, 1960).

opportunities—to the extent that they exist.[7] In low-income groups there are often several workers in one household, and family income is derived from a variety of jobs. Typically, the location of these jobs within urban areas is also varied, including manufacturing, trade, the service sectors, domestic service, and part-time casual labor.

Since the issue of housing location involves the entire urban area and not merely a few sites, the severity of the transport situation of the poor is determined primarily by city size. In the small cities walking and cycling can provide acceptable solutions for the poor almost everywhere in the urban area. The upper population limit of a city in which this is possible is about 100,000. From this size to a city with a population of about 500,000 the transport situation becomes somewhat more pressing. Mechanized transport becomes necessary, but a range of transport modes usually is available to keep the situation manageable, even for families living on the urban fringe. In cities with populations ranging from 500,000 to 2 million, the transport problem for those persons on the fringe becomes acute. The cost of long bus trips or long walking or cycling time strictly limits access of the poor to employment. Railways, subways, and related rapid-transit solutions are options worth considering, but they may involve capital outlays beyond the capacities of these cities or countries. In the twenty-three metropolitan areas with populations in the mid-1970s in excess of 2 million—five in relatively high-income countries, twelve in middle-income countries, and six in the poorest countries—transport is a serious problem for the city and particularly for the urban poor. If the poor live on the periphery and thus must travel long distances, they may not be able to afford daily work trips unless they can find employment at an intermediate location. Some are thus effectively shut off from employment in the city center; others walk up to two or three hours each way to work. Many opportunities for supplementary earning by primary earners and almost all opportunities for secondary earners may be ruled out. Efficient and diversified private transport using microbuses or jitneys can mitigate these problems somewhat. A more lasting solution, however, will usually involve the promotion of numerous decentralized employment centers to which commuting costs, by whatever means, can be kept within reach of the poor.

Low-paid jobs often are concentrated almost exclusively in city centers, especially in small cities. Even in large cities most opportunities for service jobs and other low-paid work tend to be in the commer-

7. Robert A. Hackenberg, "The Poverty Explosion: Population Increase and Income Decline in Davao City, 1972" (Davao: Davao Action Information Center, 1973).

cial centers. In the largest cities, however, similar job opportunities occur in intermediate and outer areas, since the dispersal of economic activity is in varying degree a natural consequence of growth. In such cases secondary centers for trading and commerce are established, service jobs are created that relate to the needs of residents, and home industries develop in conjunction with new urban growth.

Partly as a result of these factors, the poor do not live exclusively at the two stereotyped locations, center and periphery. In Mexico City, for example, three concentric zones in which the poor live—inner city slums, older ring of squatter settlements, and urban fringe—have been identified.[8] Nevertheless, high land prices and already high levels of crowding in more established low-income settlements often induce low-income families, particularly new arrivals, to settle at the growing periphery. They are not always worse off in these locations, for despite the high cost of transport they may be able to acquire less expensive housing than in more favored locations. To the extent that there are sufficient job opportunities near enough to make this added transport expense worthwhile, families may, on balance, benefit.

If large numbers of people are housed at a given location, their transport demands may be more easily met, with a beneficial impact on the operation of the transport network. Beyond this general point, the benefits of concentration depend on the location of economic activity and the type of employment at these locations. If job opportunities are focused at the city center, high land values will support mostly high-density white collar and similar employment. Industries cannot afford the land costs of locating in or near the center. But if economic activity is concentrated at a number of locations throughout the city, including the periphery, better coordination of employment demands with job availability is likely to be realized.

Construction cost

The proportion of housing cost allocated to construction varies considerably as a result of differences in the cost of materials and labor, construction techniques, the size of the structure, and the cost of other housing components. This, together with the fragmentariness of cost data and the uneven increase in recent construction cost, makes a meaningful analysis of comparative construction costs particularly difficult.

8. Jane Cowan Brown, *Patterns of Intra-Urban Settlement in Mexico City: An Examination of the Turner Theory* (M.A. dissertation, Cornell University, 1972).

Table 4.1. Cost of Basic Components of Residential Construction for Low- and Medium-Density Housing at Peripheral Locations in Selected Developing Countries

(*U.S. dollars a square meter, 1970 prices*)

Country	Cost component		
	Raw land	Land servicing	Basic construction
India	0.49	1.65	25.00
Iraq	0.70	2.87	35.84
Jamaica[a]	6.63	4.74	73.60
Jordan	1.40	3.18	39.69
Korea	2.25	3.97[b]	61.00[c]
Kuwait	1.68	5.19	64.86
Lebanon	4.00	2.82	32.52
Philippines	5.18	1.50	51.03
Saudi Arabia	2.77	3.87	48.41
Sri Lanka	1.00	3.36	42.33
Syria	2.41	2.58	32.25

a. Kingston.
b. Gwangju.
c. Seoul.
Source: Table A6 in the statistical appendix.

Cost components

Available data suggest that in 1970 the cost of construction ranged from about US$25 a square meter in India, which is generally regarded as having among the lowest construction costs in the world, to about US$74 a square meter in Jamaica (see Table 4.1 and Table A6 in the statistical appendix). About US$30 to US$40 a square meter was generally regarded as a medium range in most of Africa, Latin America, and Asia in 1970.

More recent cost data have been assembled for six cities—Ahmedabad, Bogotá, Hong Kong, Madras, Mexico City, and Nairobi—to obtain a sense of their relative values and of the share of raw land, land servicing, and basic construction costs in the total cost of dwellings (see Table A7 in the statistical appendix). These data confirm the wide cost range between cities and also indicate a substantial range within each city. Similar types of public housing built for low- and moderate-income families have a cost per square meter differing from 30 percent to more than 100 percent within the same city.[9] These costs relate to single-story and medium-rise structures, except in Hong Kong, where

9. See, for example, Brown, *Patterns of Intra-Urban Settlement in Mexico City.*

Table 4.2. Percentage of Cost of Basic Components of Low-Income Housing at Peripheral Locations of Selected Cities,[a] *Single-family and Multifamily Units*

Unit	Construction	Land	Land servicing
Single family	45–70	14–46	9–23
Multifamily	77–92	5–14	4–12

a. Ahmedabad, Bogotá, Hong Kong, Madras, Mexico City, and Nairobi.
Source: Table A7 in the statistical appendix.

they refer to dwelling units in high-rise buildings. The differences are explained primarily by the type of construction and the quality of finish.

As the data in Table 4.2 indicate, basic construction cost makes up the major proportion of total cost of low-income housing in these cities, whereas land servicing—roads, paths, street lighting, curbs, storm drains, and the like—accounts for minor portions of the total cost. The upper range of construction cost generally relates to moderate- and upper-income housing, with larger dwelling units and a higher quality of finish. Because raw land cost in this comparison pertains to peripheral land, it typically constitutes a lower proportion of total cost than would have been the case had intermediate or centrally located land been used.

Cost per square meter is useful as a general measure of cost differences, but it depends partly on the size of the dwelling unit and the amount of common space in multifamily buildings. The fixed costs of staircases, passages, and related common features are similar for small and large dwelling units, which implies that larger units will tend to have lower construction cost per square meter. In the six cities

Table 4.3. Basic Construction Cost per Square Meter of Livable Space in Buildings of Varying Height, Selected Cities
(*U.S. dollars, current prices*)

City	1 Story	2 Story	4 Story	High rise
Madras, 1974	20.9	34.1	52.8	78.6
Bombay, 1973	35.3	31.8	37.8	43.4
Kingston, 1970	56.3	56.3	64.7	n.a.

n.a. Not available.
Source: Madras, average cost for private development, World Bank mission, 1974; Bombay, Architects Combine, estimates from hypothetical buildings, "A Comparative Study of Low and High Rise Housing for the Low Income Group" (Bombay: The City and Industrial Development Corporation of Maharashtra Ltd., March 1973; processed); Kingston, estimates from proposals for Trench Town redevelopment project, Shankland Cox, *Low Cost Housing in Jamaica* (London: Shankland Cox and Associates, 1971).

studied, the minimum size of family units currently built varies from 20 to 50 square meters and, except in Hong Kong, the units are built in structures of from one to four stories.

There is evidence that construction cost per unit of floor area rises with the height of the building (see Table 4.3). In Colombia the construction cost per square meter of thirty-story apartments is from 40 to 60 percent above those of four- to five-story apartments and at least double those of single-family housing. In India construction cost per square meter of an eight-story apartment building is nearly double that of a four-story building.[10] Cost increases sharply, especially for high-rise structures, because of the need for elevators; higher structural cost for foundations, beams, and columns; and increases in wage rates for more skilled work and for work at heights. In contrast, the cost difference between mid- and high-rise structures tends to be smaller in developed countries and in countries with high-rise building experience.

Although unit costs tend to rise with building height, they may be virtually the same for buildings similar in construction but differing in height by only one or two stories. For example, there is usually little difference in construction cost between identical dwelling units in two- to four-story buildings or between apartments in eight- and ten-story buildings. In Manila the construction cost per square meter of four- to six-story buildings is estimated to be only about 12 percent above that of two- to three-story buildings.[11] When land price is about US$25 a square meter in India, the unit costs of two- and four-story buildings are the same.[12] And as the data in Table 4.3 suggest, unit construction cost generally is not very different for one- and two-story buildings. The increase in construction cost with the number of stories

10. W. Paul Strassmann, "Industrialized Systems Building for Developing Countries: A Discouraging Prognosis," *International Technical Cooperation Centre (ITCC) Review*, vol. 4 (January 1975), pp. 99–113. See also Architects' Combine, "A Comparative Study of Low and High Rise Housing for the Low Income Group" (Bombay: The City and Industrial Development Corporation of Maharashtra Ltd., March 1973; processed); Shankland Cox, *Low Cost Housing in Jamaica* (London: Shankland Cox and Associates, 1971); and P. A. Stone, *Urban Development in Britain: Standards, Costs and Resources, 1964–2004* (Cambridge: Cambridge University Press, 1970).

11. Development Academy of the Philippines, Housing and Urban Development Team, "Tondo Foreshore Urban Renewal Project" (Manila, May 1974; processed).

12. Strassmann, "Industrialized Systems Building," p. 107, based on R. G. Gokhale, "Some Socio-Economic Aspects of High-Rise Housing" (paper delivered at the National Conference on Tall Buildings, New Delhi, January 22–24, 1973).

Table 4.4. Indexes of Materials and Labor Costs and the Cost of Living in Mexico City, Selected Years, 1954–69

	Index			
Year	Materials cost	Labor cost	Total building cost	Workers' cost of living
1954	100.0	100.0	100.0	100.0
1959	131.2	144.1	137.3	143.5
1964	158.7	254.4	175.1	163.3
1969	184.3	328.9	209.0	189.8

Source: Dimitrios A. Germidis, *The Construction Industry in Mexico* (Paris: Organization for Economic Cooperation and Development, 1972), p. 19, from calculations based on data in "Revista Mexicana de la Construcción," May 1970.

is offset to a large extent by declines in land cost per unit, which allows some penetration of the poor into intermediate zones without reduction in construction standards.

Viewed in a dynamic sense, construction cost components vary with conditions in each construction industry and in industries producing substitute and complementary goods. In Bogotá, labor cost has risen slightly faster than overall construction cost, and the cost of most materials has risen more slowly (see Table A10 in the statistical appendix); bricks, steel, and electrical installations were exceptions, however. In Mexico City labor cost has increased much more rapidly than the average of all costs (see Table 4.4). Data for Nairobi (in Table A11 in the statistical appendix) and elsewhere suggest that the cost of skilled labor tends to rise especially rapidly. As techniques are learned and experience gained, however, overall cost should tend to fall, particularly for high-rise construction.

It is not often recognized that the planning and administration of housing can add significantly to the cost of a dwelling, particularly with high-density construction. Housing projects in Brazil, Chile, Zambia, and elsewhere have known significant arrears and outright default in rental payments. Tenant delinquencies occur principally as a result of excessively high standards that imply rents beyond the capacity of most tenants to pay and of poor rent collection and administration.[13] Attention to collection cost, but especially the design of housing

13. Barney Sheppard Rush, "From Favela to Conjunto: The Experience of Squatters Removed to Low-Cost Housing" (B. A. honors thesis, Harvard University, 1974), pp. 60–66; and W. Grindley and R. Merrill, *Sites and Services: The Experience and Potential* (Washington, D.C.: World Bank, May 1973; processed).

units within the capacity of low-income families to pay, can do much to alleviate delinquency in rental payments. In Hong Kong realistic housing standards and hence rents within the means of low-income households, together with efficient housing management, have been significant factors in the success of Hong Kong's low-income housing programs. As a result, delinquency has been negligible in Hong Kong's public housing experience.

Options in building techniques and use of labor

The construction industry is distinguished in part by its use of a wide range of materials and labor in many different combinations, the high transport cost associated with heavy or bulky materials such as timber, and the managerial capacity required to coordinate activities at the building site. Average wages in construction are generally low relative to other nonagricultural sectors, which leads in many instances to a greater use of unskilled labor and a greater labor intensiveness of production than elsewhere in the economy.

The ability to adapt to local conditions is both a characteristic of, and a necessity for, many building techniques in developing countries. The low labor costs of the clay-brick and roofing-tile industries have enabled labor-intensive methods to compete successfully in production processes that have long been mechanized in advanced countries.[14] Sites-and-services schemes and other low-income housing projects often substitute self-help for contracted labor in housing production. In some situations this may be the most efficient way to mobilize underused labor. In other cases, however, particularly in view of the institutional and administrative requirements of organizing the basic features of self-help, including access to credit and training, the hiring of contract labor to perform certain tasks may be more efficient. Self-help methods are but one means of mobilizing underused labor at close to its shadow wage, and other means—mutual help or cooperative effort, public works schemes, and contracted labor supported by organized savings plans—may usefully complement or substitute for them.

To the present, public sector self-help schemes have been successfully carried out principally for one-story dwellings. Self-help construction methods for two-story dwellings have been undertaken at private initiative with some success in countries as diverse as Peru and the United States. For buildings above two stories, however, the lim-

14. United Nations, *The Establishment of the Brick and Tile Industry in Developing Countries* (New York: U.N., 1969).

ited opportunities for incorporating self-help components into the construction of multistory buildings is a factor to be considered in housing the poor at other than peripheral locations.

Substitution possibilities among materials are also extensive. Roofs can be made of corrugated iron, roofing tile, or thatch; structure frames of timber or concrete; walls of timber, concrete blocks, clay blocks, or bricks; floors of concrete, plastic tiles, or packed earth. Soil-cement blocks and hollow concrete blocks can be made by hand or with simple machines. Such a range of options implies a wide variety of total labor inputs and of labor skills in the production of housing.

Because seasonal and various cyclical factors further complicate the process of housing production, many construction firms prefer to keep a small nucleus of managers and workers so they can expand and contract their unskilled work force in response to demand. Small firms can compete successfully with large builders if they retain this flexibility. Perhaps the principal barriers to entry for the owner-builder or the small construction firm are access to credit (often furnished by building materials merchants) and the need for liquidity to meet wage payments. Large firms may also find it easier to comply with licensing and other government procedures and often enjoy a disproportionate share of government support for public construction.

It has often been noted that building methods in many developing countries are more capital intensive than might be expected, given factor price ratios that ostensibly favor the use of labor. Consistent with objectives of labor absorption as well as of efficiency, highly labor-intensive building techniques are held to be desirable. But, some construction firms have been willing to adopt capital-using innovations even when cost comparisons would seem to indicate that relatively more labor should be used. In a housing project in Peru, for example, sand-lime bricks made with imported machinery replaced traditional handmade bricks even though they eventually cost 26.5 percent more.[15]

Part of the explanation for this capital intensiveness lies in the calculation of full production cost at market prices, a necessity for construction firms of all sizes if the market is highly competitive. Workers may in fact be less than fully productive on the job because of hunger, ill health, or lack of skills. Minimum wages and other labor market restrictions suggest that wage rates may in some cases be above the productivity of labor—especially in construction, in which productivity has grown more slowly than in most other sectors in many developing

15. W. Paul Strassmann, "Innovation and Employment in Building: The Experience of Peru," *Oxford Economic Papers*, vol. 22 (July 1970), p. 248.

countries. Labor-intensive projects may also take longer to complete. In the Peru project the greater regularity of the sand-lime bricks permitted a saving in labor and plaster for the dwelling walls that more than offset their higher cost.

When inputs are valued in social terms, however, a quite different set of priorities may emerge. Capital-intensive techniques may be used because overvalued exchange rates, subsidized interest rates, and other distortions in the economy create a structure of protection that encourages their use. Labor-intensive building projects, on the other hand, can have important multiplier effects throughout the economy that lead to improvements in such aspects of urban life as education and health. Furthermore, the very advantage to firms of being able to mobilize labor on short notice is a disadvantage to workers, who dislike the insecurity of construction employment. It is sometimes difficult to retain skilled labor and managers in construction, since their opportunities in other industries may be more attractive. Stabilization policies to counteract construction cycles can contribute to a more effective housing program.

Social valuation of housing inputs is therefore an important tool in exploring ways to reduce construction cost. Prefabrication, for example, may not be cheaper than standard construction materials in economies having a labor surplus, although in a few situations prefabricated materials may deteriorate more slowly and therefore be cheaper in the long run. Industrialized systems building such as prefabrication may use techniques requiring as little as one-third the labor force needed for traditional methods, but it usually involves heavy start-up costs in a large plant. A return to the use of traditional materials and the adaptation of new techniques to traditional building methods may be a more socially beneficial way of lowering costs, particularly in low-income countries. For example, although secondary timbers in tropical countries may not be sufficiently durable for building in their natural state, they will withstand climate and predators if appropriately treated. Small, local firms may have an advantage in producing and transporting these and other heavy items that cannot be carried economically over long distances and for which the cost of holding inventories is high. They may also be better suited to supply items on short notice. Traditional brick- and tilemaking methods may not be able to use more than a small fraction of local clays, but a more complex refractory technique may do so without abolishing labor-intensive production. Savings can be made by the use of lime, which is plentiful near many cities, instead of cement. A combination of prefabrication and traditional methods may be the most effective means of realizing the comparative advantage of each. Roofs in India may be precast, for example, but insulation is added at the site in the form of earth mixed with rice husks—an effective thermal insulator in hot climates.[16]

Few countries have conscientiously explored the possibility of reducing the cost of residential construction at various heights and levels of density. Among those which have, India is notable for its success in lowering the costs of construction through technological adaptation and rediscovery of the uses of traditional materials.[17] In economies with a labor surplus this is a rational choice. Many countries have wisely not adopted innovations that are labor conserving rather than labor using, as seems to have been the case for the majority of recent innovations in building techniques.[18]

Financial resources

Investment in urban housing involves purchase of land, construction of dwellings, and the provision of associated physical and social services. To this end, some infrastructure investment, as well as housebuilding, is usually undertaken by public agencies. Most housing investment, however, is undertaken by private agents financed from private savings.

The financing of housing, like that of any durable asset, is facilitated by a system that efficiently mediates funds from surplus economic agents to deficit units (builders and buyers of houses). And, as in the production of other assets with relatively long useful lives, house construction is aided by the availability of long-term credit.

Since housing is a durable good, it yields value beyond the year in which it is built. Financing of house purchase thus involves long-term commitments by lenders to a highly nonliquid form of wealth. Dwellings are subject also to fluctuations in value quite apart from ordinary wear and tear on the physical structure. Changes in the surrounding neighborhood and in public service networks can alter the value of a house in much the same way as changes in the amount of living space the house provides. Lenders therefore demand compensation for the

16. V. Malakonda Reddy and A. S. Sarma, "Construction Methods for Low-Cost Housing," *Proceedings of the International Symposium on Low Cost Housing Problems Related to Urban Renewal and Development* (Rolla, Missouri: University of Missouri–Rolla, October 1970).

17. See Government of Kerala, Report of Expert Committee, *Performance Approach to Cost Reduction in Building Construction* (Trivandrum, January 1974).

18. W. Paul Strassmann, "Industrialized Systems Building," pp. 111–12.

risk involved in housing finance, a risk that they often feel is greater for low-income families.

Housing finance in developing countries suffers from disabilities that are common to all types of long-term finance and from those which are specific to housing. In most developing countries, financial systems are underdeveloped and beset by government restrictions that limit the volume of long-term finance and distort its allocation. Financial systems typically are dominated by commercial banks that base their practice on nineteenth-century Anglo-Saxon banking principles and lend on terms that technically require repayment in a short period. The proportion of mortgages and other long-term loans is kept low. Points of view that interpret usury as an evil have often led to the pegging of commercial bank interest rates at artificially low levels, thereby hampering the ability of the banks to attract funds. With excessive demand thus created by controlled interest rates, banks prefer lending to the least risky borrowers, and what little mortgage money is made available is channeled to rich customers with ample collateral. Low-income families, and often those with medium incomes, are excluded in such a rationing. Alternative sources of long-term institutional finance are scarce and operate under many of the same restrictions. Life insurance companies, pension funds, and savings banks, which are important providers of long-term housing finance in developed countries, are generally newborn institutions in developing countries and have small portfolios. They also are often subject to interest rate ceilings, which act to limit the stock of long-term funds mediated for all purposes, including housing, and to tilt its allocation in favor of the rich. Low-income families are left to rely on the informal credit market, in which interest rates are often four times their level elsewhere, or to a few mutual savings associations.

Hindrances specific to housing finance also exist. Because in the past investment in housing has often been labeled "unproductive" by governments that have failed to understand its economic significance, legal restrictions have sometimes been deployed. Commercial banks in Turkey, for example, are not permitted to make mortgage loans. Elsewhere the opposite view—that housing is a basic need to be supplied at a low price—has inspired low ceilings for interest rates on mortgage loans. This not only has resulted in a small volume of mortgage business being undertaken by existing intermediaries but also has curbed the growth of life insurance companies, which need the existence of remunerative and safe long-term assets for their development. Some governments have created specialized mortgage institutions financed by concessionary public funds—by, for example, earmarked payroll taxes—to meet this basic need. Since such funds are severely limited, however, stringent rationing to borrowers has necessarily been imposed.

Examples of this process include, in Latin America, the Brazilian housing bank known as BNH and the Mexican national workers' housing institute (Instituto del Fondo Nacional de la Vivienda para los Trabajadores, or INFONAVIT). The former institution extended loans in the past only to families with the equivalent of at least four minimum salaries. By mid-1975 these conditions had been relaxed, allowing some loans to go to families below the old cutoff point. The latter by the mid-1970s was also trying to liberalize such procedures by moving toward provision of two-thirds of its loans to workers earning between one and one-and-a-half minimum salaries.

A study of housing in Africa concluded as early as the mid-1960s that housing finance fails to reach low-income groups,[19] but change has proved immensely difficult to implement. In 1967 the official newspaper of the Ivory Coast reported that Crédit de Côte d'Ivoire, a semi-public enterprise, gave 50 percent of its loans for housing to those of "très bon standing," and the other 50 percent to housing corporations producing expensive apartments and to middle-income families. Of all the credit provided by public institutions, less than 10 percent was given to individuals.[20]

In these circumstances housing finance can benefit from reform that seeks to improve the workings of financial markets. A general freeing of interest rate restrictions, the enactment of measures to encourage competition among banks, the erosion of inappropriate banking traditions, and the promotion of life insurance companies and pension funds would all increase the availability of long-term credit and potentially provide financing for an efficient housing sector. Admittedly, increased competition among financial intermediaries need not always increase the availability of finance for housing: in a few developing countries in which savings banks with large mortgage portfolios are protected from deposit competition from the commercial banks, the removal of this protection could reduce the deposit base of the savings banks and their mortgage business. More generally, however, the removal of specific hindrances to housing finance would allow housing to compete effectively with other claimants for long-term institutional finance.

These reforms of the financial system can be expected to increase the quantity and quality of financial intermediation and to reduce the

19. United Nations, *Housing in Africa* (New York: U.N., 1965).
20. *Fraternité Hebdomadaire*, December 1, 1967, p. 12.

biases against long-term credit in general and housing finance in particular. Within such a market, and depending on the size of the market, separate housing finance institutions can develop to provide specialized intermediation services at lower costs.

A more controversial issue is raised by the question of whether the financial system should be endowed with biases in favor of housing finance. Broadly speaking, housing finance could be favored in two ways: by the application of various selective credit policies to divert more funds to housing; and by supporting housing finance with subsidy from the public sector or foreign aid. The most common example of the first category has been the channeling of funds mobilized by compulsory social security systems for housing. In general, however, the use of these funds has been confined to contributors, which limits access to these highly subsidized resources to upper echelons of factory workers, public service employees, and other middle- and upper-income groups. The experience of countries as widely different as Iran and the Philippines indicates that such policies clearly augment housing finance to these groups—but low-income groups are left out. In the Philippines the Government Service Insurance System and the Social Security System grant mortgage loans for construction to qualified recipients. Although these institutions have attempted to design a number of projects that would cater to low-income families, their programs do not generally promote low-income housing as a special concern. Under the institutional arrangements that have prevailed to date, only a small portion of loanable funds has accrued to low-income families.

Other methods of supporting housing finance include the provision of subsidized lines of discount for housing by central banks and the imposition of portfolio restrictions on commercial banks, which, as in Mexico, gives these institutions an incentive to favor housing in their lending. As with other administrative channeling of funds, however, these policies beg the question of whether the resources could not have been used more productively in other activities.

There are several arguments in favor of providing public subsidies or concessionary foreign credits to promote specialized housing finance institutions. First, such an institution (it is argued) can provide housing for the poor who cannot otherwise afford to obtain the necessary finance. Second, a specialized institution with deposit facilities may induce savings from people for whom believable prospects for home ownership constitute a distinct saving incentive and for whom such prospects are convincingly heightened by the existence of the institution. This motivation may be particularly important for low-income groups, who are generally rationed out of housing loans by the standard intermediaries. Third, it is often held that more planned and rational housing can be achieved by linking the financial institution with the public authority responsible for zoning and setting building standards. This might allow setting and implementation of maximum building standards in place of the more common minimum standards operating in developed countries.

The reduction of imperfections in housing finance is never easy, but in a situation of housing shortage the difficulties of reaching the poor by providing housing finance—even at subsidized rates—are especially acute. The main effect of subsidy-supported housing finance institutions is likely to be an increase in the supply of funds for middle-income housing. Therefore, whether it is desirable to promote specialized housing finance institutions through subsidies must be determined largely by evaluating, first, the external benefits that can be derived in the form of facilitating better urban planning, and, second, the stimulus that these institutions can provide to small savers.

Five

Demand

AS THE FOREGOING CHAPTERS DEMONSTRATE, housing gives families an opportunity to be more productive, thereby conferring greater benefits on the entire economy. A logical conclusion often drawn is that each family consequently requires—and should be assured—a specified minimal standard of housing services. Although well intentioned, programs having this objective stand little chance of success if they are not carried out with a realistic assessment of what families can afford to pay for housing. By comparing housing costs with the capacity of families to meet reasonable monthly payments, this chapter argues for strategies based on the effective demand for housing.

Housing need and effective demand

The conception "housing need" embraces the total requirement for shelter, without consideration of whether or not families can pay for it. Definitions of such need may be expressed as a minimum quality of structure required, a maximum rate of occupancy (fewer than three persons a room, for example), or an upper limit on the proportion of income spent for housing. The definitions include less often a minimum of privacy and security or the distance beyond which travel to work becomes too costly. More than one of these needs may be unsatisfied simultaneously. A household may, for example, live in a dilapidated house, in overcrowded conditions, and still be paying more than 25 percent of its income in rent.

61

In contrast, the effective demand for housing is derived from each household's willingness to pay for housing. The level of household income, its distribution, and the prices of available housing and of other goods and services are important influences on decisions about how much to spend on housing. So are demographic patterns and the particular constitution of the household, which determine the growth of demand over time. Each family must assign a priority to housing, the amount it is willing to pay, in relation to other items in the household budget.

Most attempts to establish housing programs that have failed to distinguish adequately between need and effective demand have had little success. Need is often determined from such readily available statistics as the number of households living in slums, then is translated into the investment required to satisfy the need. The resulting numbers are so huge as to nourish the seeds of hopelessness. More important, such an approach is seriously misleading. Since relative income, structural housing conditions, overcrowding, and housing costs vary with (among other factors) a city's level of development, income distribution, rate of urbanization, and climate, it is difficult to compare housing need between cities. The minimal four-room dwelling unit of a cabinetmaker in Bogotá, with electricity, water, and sewerage, will appear an unattainable luxury to a cabinetmaker in Calcutta. The approach also fails to consider alternatives that attempt to mobilize latent or underused purchasing power. Policymakers should seek first to convert measures of housing need into those of effective demand.

In establishing such measures, the nature of the tradeoffs involved and the provision of alternative housing options for low-income families in urban areas of widely varying characteristics must be taken into account. Families usually have at least the notional choice between (a) relatively roomy and good-quality shelter at locations with poor and costly access to income-earning opportunities and (b) cramped living conditions in locations with good access. To determine the demand schedules for housing by various income groups it would be necessary, first, to define the range of housing choices or packages of components available; second, to establish the economic cost or rental value of each choice; and, third, to determine the quantity of each type of housing demanded at the prevailing rent. Choices would then be specified according to their location (with respect, particularly, to employment opportunities, but also to the other services and amenities offered by a city), to transport services available at the location and their cost, to the size and quality of the dwelling unit, and to the utilities and other services available.

To generate even an approximation of these choices within a city would require reasonably reliable data on the land market, employment location within the city, point-to-point transport costs in time and money, construction costs, and infrastructure costs as a function of distance and density. This approach would then abstract from all but the principal feature of housing location (in most cases, access to employment opportunities) and would therefore implicitly assume that education, health, police and fire protection, and other services are equally available at all locations. All costs would have to be expressed in social as well as market accounting prices.

In practice the data are always limited. For example, information about employment locations and point-to-point transport opportunities and costs is nowhere available in the necessary detail. The analyst must work with a limited picture of land values, infrastructure costs, and construction costs for different types of structures. In the analysis that follows, a limited approach has been adopted based on private rather than social costs (or crudely adjusted private costs in some circumstances) and on estimates of demand based on the assignment of a fixed proportion of income to housing.

Housing cost and income

The overriding urban housing problem is easy to pinpoint: the inadequacy of incomes of large numbers of households to pay for the housing that is currently being produced. But the income-cost relation is less simple to document and analyze. First, although absolute levels of income have a large impact on demand, income relative to that of neighbors, friends, and co-workers is also important. As will be documented below, the distribution of income of a city as a whole will affect the affordability of housing to different income groups. Furthermore, noneconomic factors such as tastes and preferences—for certain types of building materials or finish, for open space to grow vegetables or keep chickens, for communal kitchen facilities—can be important in many cultural and political environments. Consequently, there is a great variation in the proportion of urban households served and in the differences between the market price of housing and family resources available to spend on housing.

Although the average cost of housing—the cost per square meter of floor space—is one measure of its affordability, the total cost of the dwelling is the more important factor when trying to reach the poor, since this is the cost the poor must pay. In the six cities studied, the economic cost (without subsidy or profit and before financing cost) of the cheapest new dwelling varies from a low of US$570 in Madras to a high of US$3,005 in Mexico City in 1970 prices—as shown in Table 5.1.

Table 5.1. Cost and Quality of the Cheapest Housing Unit Currently Provided by the Public Sector, Selected Cities[a]

City	Cost of cheapest housing unit (U.S. dollars, 1970 prices)	Area (square meters)		Percent distribution of component cost			Location	Type of unit
		Housing unit	Land	Raw land	Land servicing	Basic construction		
Ahmedabad	616	20.0	20	7.3	8.6	84.1	Periphery	In four-story flat
Bogotá	1,475	50.0	75	18.3	12.2	69.5	Periphery	Single-family detached house
Hong Kong	1,670	18.0	n.a.	33.9	66.1		Periphery, satellite community	High-rise one-room flat; cost includes share of community facilities
Madras	570	17.5	50	28.9	23.0	48.1	Periphery	Single-family detached house
Mexico City	3,005	47.3	186	45.8	9.3	44.9	Periphery	Single-family detached house
Nairobi	2,076	20.5	150	14.0	21.5	64.5	Periphery	Core house with one room

n.a. Not available.

a. With individual toilet and services. Year of construction varies from 1970 to 1974 (see Table A13 in the statistical appendix). Excludes some administrative cost, interest during construction, and certain costs arising from rental delinquency or default.

Source: Derived from Table A13 in the statistical appendix.

A rough preliminary indication of how these costs compare with household incomes in the cities studied can be obtained using the rule of thumb often adopted in developed countries: that a family generally should not purchase a dwelling whose cost is more than 2.5 times annual income. These comparisons, reported in Table 5.2, indicate that for the average income of the city as a whole, the costs of the cheapest units available are well within these informal guidelines. But comparisons with the median incomes of the lowest 40 percent and 20 percent of households show that even the cheapest new dwellings are within reach only if these groups severely distort their overall expenditure patterns by spending much less on other items. Hong Kong, Bogotá, and Madras are exceptions for the lowest 40 percent of households; and Hong Kong is an exception down to the 20 percent level. Families in Nairobi's lowest quintile wishing to purchase such a dwelling would have to pay an amount more than seven times annual income. This rule-of-thumb type of guideline is useful to generalize about housing affordability, but it must be supplemented by more detailed cost and income comparisons.

The average percentage of household expenditure devoted to housing, shown for several cities in Table 5.3, falls into a fairly narrow range, from 11.7 percent in Kingston to about 20 percent in Mexico City and Seoul. Generalizations relating average expenditure on housing to the population and employment patterns of different cities are, of course, not possible with this small sample. It should also be reemphasized that because of variations in the definitions of housing expenditures—especially whether utilities, furnishings, and taxes are included or not—cross-country comparisons of expenditure are extremely hazardous. Given this caveat, the data in Table 5.3 seem to suggest that variations in average expenditure have no observable relation to the countries' national income per capita.

The fragmentary data available on expenditure by various income groups, however, indicate a general tendency for housing expenditure by low-income households to claim a higher than average share. Distortions in expenditure for housing as well as other items seem to be widespread at low income levels, but they differ in severity and impact from city to city. Further comparisons—for example, of tradeoffs among expenditures on housing, utilities, and transport at various income levels—are unfortunately not possible because of insufficient reliable and comparable information.

Certain broad trends may nevertheless be deduced (see Table 5.4). Except for Korean and Indian cities, housing expenditure appears to be either a roughly constant or a gradually decreasing function of income. As income rises and other demands are met, the share of income de-

Table 5.2. Cost of Cheapest Housing Unit as Percent of Annual Household Income, Selected Cities, 1970

City	Cost of cheapest complete housing unit (U.S. dollars, 1970 prices)	Annual household income			Cost of housing unit as percent of		
		Average	Median, lowest 40 percent	Median, lowest 20 percent	Average	Median, lowest 40 percent	Median, lowest 20 percent
Ahmedabad	616	540	216	96	114.1	285.2	641.7
Bogotá	1,475	2,052	612	432	71.8	240.8	341.4
Hong Kong	1,670	2,136	980	672	78.2	170.4	248.5
Madras	570	420	228	192	135.7	250.0	296.9
Mexico City	3,005	2,892	1,020	828	103.9	294.6	362.9
Nairobi	2,076	2,100	468	288	98.9	443.6	720.8

Source: Derived from Tables A13 through A15 in the statistical appendix.

Table 5.3. Comparison of National Income per Capita with Percentage of Household Expenditure on Housing, Selected Cities, Various Years

Country and city[a]	Year	National income per capita, 1970 (U.S. dollars)	Average percentage of household expenditure on housing
Hong Kong		970	
Hong Kong	1973		15.1
Singapore		920	
Singapore	1973		19.5[b]
Mexico		670	
Mexico City	1973		20.0[c]
Jamaica		670	
Kingston	1963–64		11.7[d]
Korea			
All cities	1972		18.5
Seoul	1972		20.1
Philippines		210	
All cities	1971		12.5
Manila[e]	1971		18.0
India		110	
Calcutta	1971		15.0[f]
Zaïre		90	
Kinshasa	1970		13.5
Bukavu	1971		13.5
Kisangani	1972		11.9

a. In descending order of national income per capita.
b. Rentals in Housing Board flats, including utilities, as percentage of household income.
c. Rough average of rent or amortization as percentage of household income for low- to middle-income families.
d. Working-class urban households.
e. Metropolitan area.
f. Rent and taxes paid as a percentage of household income for low-income families with total incomes up to US$300 a year.
Source: World Bank data obtained or compiled from various national sources.

voted to housing may remain constant or fall.[1] Expenditure on utilities tends to decline with income in every city studied. For transport the

1. The income elasticity of demand for housing appears to be, at most, unity. Recent estimates have suggested that, even when lifetime income is used, this elasticity is likely to be less than unity. See W. Paul Strassmann, "Measuring the Employment Effects of Housing Policies in Developing Countries," *Economic Development and Cultural Change* (forthcoming); Geoffrey Carliner, "Income Elasticity of Housing Demand," *Review of Economics and Statistics*, vol. 55 (November 1973), pp. 528–32; Margaret G. Reid, *Housing and Income* (Chicago: University of Chicago Press, 1962); Richard F. Muth, *Cities and Housing* (Chicago: University of Chicago Press, 1969); and R. K. Wilkinson, "The Income Elasticity of Demand for Housing," *Oxford Economic Papers*, vol. 25 (November 1973), pp. 361–77.

Table 5.4. Household Income and Percentage of Household Expenditure on Housing, Utilities, and Transport, Selected Cities, Various Years

Country, city, and year	Monthly household income (U.S. dollars)	Percentage of expenditure on Housing	Percentage of expenditure on Utilities[a]	Percentage of expenditure on Transport
Colombia: Bogotá, 1972	0.0–23.8	59.3[b]	6.8	4.9[c]
	23.9–47.6	24.1	3.3	3.9
	47.7–71.4	23.1	3.5	5.3
	71.5–95.2	21.9	2.7	2.8
	95.3–142.8	22.7	2.8	3.7
	142.9–238.1	26.6	3.0	4.0
	238.2–809.5	24.4	1.9	5.2
	809.6 and over	22.0	1.5	12.9
Hong Kong, 1973	80.8–303.0	19.8[b]	3.1	4.0
	303.1–606.7	18.4	2.7	4.9
India: Bombay, Calcutta, Delhi, and Madras, 1964	0.0–2.70	6.2[d]	n.a.	1.2
	2.71–3.10	2.5	n.a.	0.6
	3.11–3.75	2.8	n.a.	1.3
	3.76–4.38	4.3	n.a.	1.9
	4.39–5.00	3.4	n.a.	2.0
	5.01–5.84	3.7	n.a.	1.4
	5.85–7.09	5.2	n.a.	1.9
	7.10–8.97	5.8	n.a.	3.1
	8.98–11.47	5.3	n.a.	3.1
	11.48–15.64	5.0	n.a.	2.9
	15.65 and over	7.6	n.a.	5.6
Kenya: Nairobi, 1968	0.0–28.0	46.0	n.a.	n.a.
	28.1–42.0	22.0	n.a.	n.a.
	42.1–70.0	15.0	n.a.	n.a.
	70.1–140.0	12.5	n.a.	n.a.
	140.1–280.0	18.5	n.a.	n.a.
	280.1 and over	15.0	n.a.	n.a.
Korea: all cities, 1970	0.0–44.4	18.1[b]	10.6	3.6[c]
	44.5–74.0	16.5	8.6	4.6
	74.1–103.7	16.9	6.8	4.7
	103.8–133.3	17.3	5.7	4.4
	133.4–162.9	18.2	5.4	5.0
	163.0–192.6	18.2	5.0	4.3
	192.7 and over	19.6	4.7	5.6

n.a. Not available.
a. Includes fuel and electricity.
b. Private housing.
c. Purchase and use of transport services and personal equipment.
d. Includes rent and expenditure on repair and maintenance; excludes land purchase.

Sources: Colombia, Departamento Administrativo Nacional de Estadísticas (Bogotá, 1972; Hong Kong, Hong Kong Census and Statistics Department, *1973/74 Household Expenditure Survey;* India, Government of India, *The National Sample Survey, 19th Round, July 1964–June 1965: Tables with Notes on Consumer Expenditure* (New Delhi: Cabinet Secretariat, 1971); Kenya, *Urban Household Expenditure Survey 1968–69;* Korea, *Annual Report on the Family Income and Expenditure Survey* (Seoul: Economic Planning Board, 1970).

pattern is less clear. Apart from a sharp increase in the highest income bracket, which appears to be largely the result of private automobile ownership, variations in transport expenditure with income depend heavily on city-specific features such as street networks, congestion, and the availability of public transport.

Because surveys of family spending patterns are usually not repeated at regular intervals, comparisons of household expenditures over time are extremely difficult. A notable exception is the series of annual surveys conducted by the Economic Planning Board of Korea. Results for 1968 through 1972—summarized in appendix Table A16 for Seoul and for all other urban areas in Korea—show that the average expenditure on housing has risen slightly over this five-year period; the outlay on utilities and transport has remained roughly constant.

These patterns of expenditure by income class and the number of households in each income category produce an income distribution for the city against which the cost of currently built housing may be compared. The distribution of households by income classes in the cities studied shows considerable variation (see Tables A14 and A15 in the statistical appendix). Generally, the median income of the lowest 40 percent is less than one-quarter the average income. By comparing income distributions with housing costs, a measure is obtained of the proportion of households that can be housed without subsidy in dwellings presently built. The data available on economic cost of the cheapest currently built dwelling produced by the public sector in each city were used to make a reasonably realistic test of what is possible under present conditions.[2] In this analysis, households were assumed to spend 15 percent of their income on housing and to have no down payment and twenty-five years to repay. (These assumptions represent a reasonable range of financing programs in low-income housing.)

The data summarized in Table 5.5 show the percent of total urban households unable to afford the cheapest new housing unit, assuming no down payment and a twenty-five–year repayment period, at interest rates of 10 and 15 percent. At a 10 percent interest rate, 68 percent of households in Nairobi, 64 percent in Ahmedabad, 63 percent in Madras, 55 percent in Mexico City, and 47 percent in Bogotá have insufficient income to afford the cheapest dwelling; in Hong Kong the figure is 35 percent. Thus, present housing policies exclude not only the poor but also many middle-income families. Unable to obtain the package of housing services they would prefer, middle-income households are forced into housing that the poor would otherwise have occupied.

2. The assumption that these dwellings can be produced in any number at constant cost is probably unrealistic in the short run, though more tenable in the long run.

Table 5.5. Estimates of Monthly Household Income Required to Purchase the Cheapest Existing New Housing Unit[a] and the Percentage of Households Unable to Afford It, at Varying Interest Rates, Selected Cities

City	Cost of cheapest housing unit (U.S. dollars, 1970 prices)	Interest rate of 10 percent			Interest rate of 15 percent		
		Monthly payment[b,c]	Monthly household income required[c,d]	Percentage of households unable to afford	Monthly payment[b,c]	Monthly household income required[c,d]	Percentage of households unable to afford
Ahmedabad	616	5.6	38	64	8.7	58	79
Bogotá	1,475	13.6	91	47	19.0	127	61
Hong Kong	1,670	15.4	103	35	21.5	143	57
Madras	570	5.3	36	63	7.3	49	79
Mexico City	3,005	27.6	184	55	38.8	259	66
Nairobi	2,076	19.1	127	68	26.8	178	77

a. With individual toilet and services. Excludes some administrative cost, interest during construction, and certain costs arising from rental delinquency or default. Hong Kong figures include administrative and maintenance costs.
b. Assuming repayment period of twenty-five years.
c. Figures represent 1970 prices except for Hong Kong (1971) and Mexico City (1969).
d. Assuming no down payment and 15 percent of household income devoted to housing.
Source: Tables A13 and A14 in the statistical appendix.

These results are sensitive to changes in the terms on which housing can be purchased. If the interest rate is 15 percent, an additional 9 to 22 percent of households have insufficient incomes. Less than half of Hong Kong households can afford housing on these terms, compared with 65 percent at the lower interest rate. In Ahmedabad and Madras four-fifths of the city's households are not served if the interest rate is 15 percent. Furthermore, if allowance were made for other costs likely to be incurred and not fully coverable in the estimates (collection costs of monthly payments and other administrative costs, maintenance costs, allowances for default and interest during construction, and the like), the proportion of the population unable to afford the cheapest new housing would be even greater. Only for Hong Kong did the available data permit an approximately full coverage of costs.

Whatever the interest rate or repayment terms, reduction of housing costs to levels attainable by the urban poor is imperative. To assess the effects of decreases in total housing costs—leaving aside for the moment how these decreases might be realized—hypothetical cost reductions of 10 percent, 20 percent, and one-third were applied to the above cost figures. These and subsequent comparisons assume an interest rate of 10 percent. The additional percentage of households that would be reached depends on the distribution of income and on the level of present costs, as shown in Table 5.6. Figure 5.1, in which income distribution is illustrated for the cities studied, also indicates the percentage unable to afford the new housing at present costs and with a 10 percent reduction. A 20 percent cost reduction, for example, would enable the market to reach an additional 18 percent of households in Madras but only an extra 5 percent in Nairobi.

The data in Table 5.6 also indicate what cost reductions are required to reach all but the lowest 40 percent, 20 percent, and 10 percent of urban households. Cost reductions to reach the bottom 40 percent range from zero in Hong Kong, where all but 35 percent are currently served, to 50 percent in Nairobi. Cost reductions to reach the bottom 20 percent are 23 percent in Hong Kong and 69 percent in Nairobi. To serve all but the lowest decile, costs would have to be reduced by about 80 percent in Nairobi but only 45 percent in Hong Kong. This latter reduction—in fact more—is now achieved in Hong Kong through land price write-downs and interest subsidies. In such a situation the relatively small number of households involved makes the provision of subsidies financially feasible.

The methods by which reductions of this kind can be achieved thus become an important issue. First, and most simply, reduced building standards can lower the dwelling cost to each household. Indigenous materials and traditional building methods can be substituted for

Table 5.6. Reduction of Housing Cost and the Percentage of Households that Can Be Served, Selected Cities[a]

City	Percentage of households unable to afford lowest-cost housing unit				Percentage reduction of present cost required to reach all but lowest		
	At present cost	At 10 percent reduction	At 20 percent reduction	At one-third reduction	40 percent	20 percent	10 percent
Ahmedabad	64	58	56	51	41.9	52.3	78.9
Bogotá	47	42	37	26	13.8	43.2	60.2
Hong Kong	35	30	22	14	0	22.6	45.3
Madras	63	52	45	31	25.6	44.7	54.2
Mexico City	55	52	47	37	28.4	53.7	62.4
Nairobi	68	66	63	53	49.8	69.1	81.2

a. Assuming 15 percent of household income devoted to housing, a repayment period of twenty-five years, no down payment, and 10 percent interest.
Source: Tables A13 and A14 in the statistical appendix.

Figure 5.1. Distribution of Monthly Household Income and Housing Affordability, Selected Cities

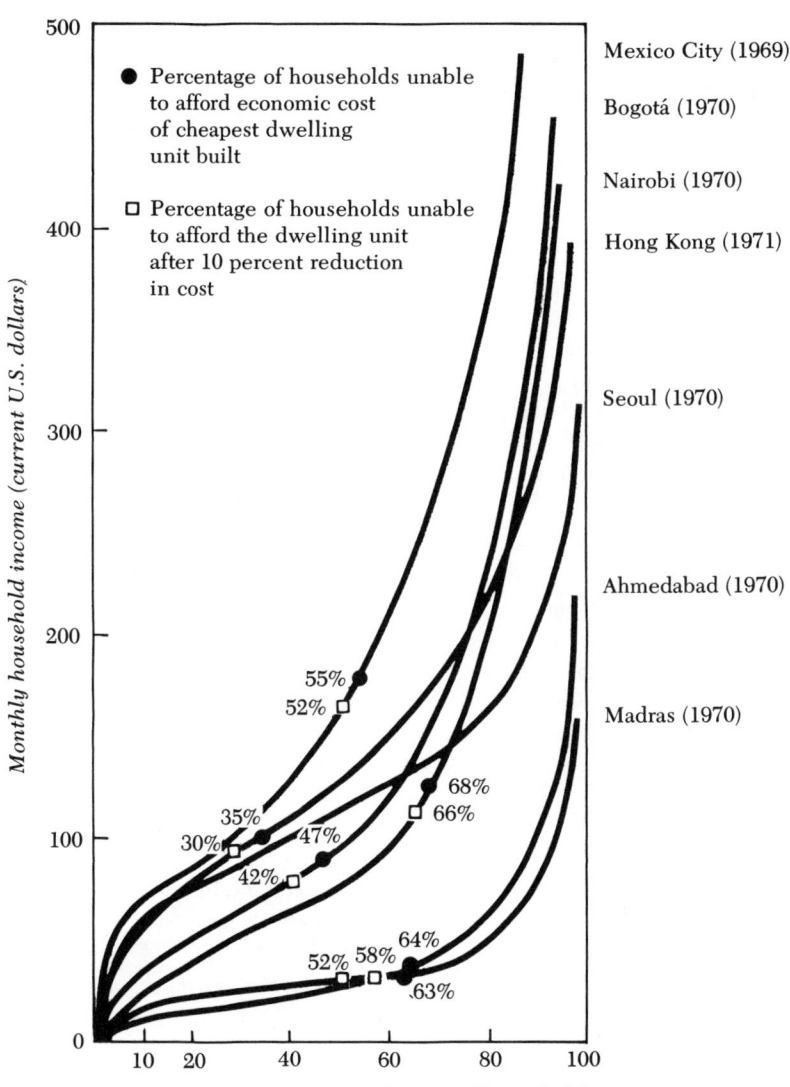

Cumulative percentage distribution of households

Sources: Tables A13 and A14 in the statistical appendix.

higher-cost materials, and a lower quality of finish can be accepted. Second, lower service levels—the sharing of latrines, kitchens, and other facilities, for example—can have an important impact on cost. Substantial savings can also result from reducing the land area devoted to each dwelling: for example, by constructing row houses that share walls on both sides or four- to six-story walk-up apartment buildings. Alternative methods for cost reduction involve tradeoffs (a) between single-family and multifamily structures and (b) between self-help methods to use labor with low opportunity cost and multistory formal construction to use land more efficiently and reduce its weight in total dwelling cost.

These tradeoffs have to be taken into account in housing decisions. Because the full range of data for such decisions was not available, all the options cannot be detailed here. But an illustration of what could be accomplished through the selective reduction of various costs can be provided in a schematic exercise using data from the cities studied and varying assumptions about space standards and quality of service. Four features that can be affected by public policy have been isolated for analysis: livable space per household, land area per household, public service levels, and location. The range of variation of each feature was as follows:

Livable space per household
▫ 20 square meters
▫ 10 square meters

Service levels
▫ Individual (individual water supply,
  sewage disposal, toilet)
▫ Shared (cooking, toilet, and other services
  shared among small family groups)
▫ Basic (centrally located water and pit
  latrines, minimal security lighting, and site preparation)

Land area per household
▫ 75 square meters, single-family detached dwelling
▫ 15 square meters, share, four-story walk-up

Location
▫ Center of city (central business district commercial property)
▫ Intermediate zone (approximately one-third
  the distance to periphery)
▫ Periphery (limits of urbanized area)

These comparisons take as their point of departure the actual costs of the cheapest single-family and multifamily public housing units currently built in the cities studied. Hypothetical reductions in the costs of these units were calculated on the basis of the following assumptions: first, that interior livable space would be reduced to 20 square meters per dwelling unit; second, that gross densities would be increased by associated changes in land-use standards; third, that reductions in the cost of services and construction would follow three different service level standards: individual, shared, and basic; and, fourth, that all costs would be calculated on the basis of land prices currently prevailing at each location. The effects of change in location are examined using land prices at the city center, at intermediate locations (defined, as noted above, as one-third the distance from center to periphery), and at the periphery. Total dwelling costs are compared with the monthly payments required to amortize the purchase at 10 percent interest for twenty-five years, and this required monthly payment is translated into annual income, assuming that 15 percent of household income is devoted to housing. Comparison of this figure with each income distribution shows the number of households that can and cannot afford each type and quality of dwelling.

The results are presented in appendix Tables A17 through A21 and summarized in Table 5.7. Not all the elements of this matrix will, of course, necessarily be practical: few if any housing policies, for example, would include pit latrines in central city locations. Nevertheless, it is desirable to present all permutations for exposition of the full range of public housing alternatives.

The data presented in Table 5.7 point up the crucial weight of land costs in the total cost of a dwelling and hence in its affordability, if construction costs can be lowered to the extent postulated by a reduction of livable space and a sharing of services. In Bogotá, for example, single-family dwellings with shared services could reach all but 14 percent of households if the dwellings were located at the periphery. The same standard dwelling in intermediate zones would become too costly for nearly three-quarters of the population because of higher land costs. Multifamily dwellings and lower standards at the intermediate location would still not reach 40 percent of the population. These differences seem to be more pronounced in the higher-income cities than in Madras, in which single-family dwellings with shared services would serve only 5 percent fewer households in intermediate zones than at the periphery. By extension, in all but very low-income cities the most highly valued land in the city—commercial property at the city center—is excluded from the poor no matter what level of living standards and services is provided.

Similar conclusions are reached from a somewhat different angle by calculating the level of subsidy, if any, implied by these housing alternatives. One measure of the implied subsidy—the amount (in percentage) by which monthly incomes available for housing fall short of re-

Table 5.7. *Estimates of Cost of Housing Units of Various Standards and Locations and Percentage of Households Unable to Afford Them, Selected Cities*
(*Cost in U.S. dollars, 1970 prices*)

Type of housing[a]	Ahmedabad Cost	Percent	Bogotá Cost	Percent	Hong Kong[b] Cost	Percent	Madras Cost	Percent	Mexico City Cost	Percent	Nairobi Cost	Percent
1. Present cheapest housing unit	616	64	1,475	47	1,670	35	570	63	3,005	55	2,076	68
Periphery												
2. Single family, individual services[c]	531	58	754	17	d	d	747	77	1,243	14	1,860	66
3. Single family, shared services[e]	469	56	665	14	d	d	670	73	1,117	10	1,566	59
4. Single family, basic services[f]	408	51	576	11	d	d	592	68	991	6	1,272	52
5. Multifamily, individual services	605	64	1,086	36	1,734	38	651	70	1,181	12	1,836	65
6. Multifamily, shared services	491	58	884	23	1,568	32	541	65	975	7	1,496	58
7. Multifamily, basic services	377	41	681	15	1,402	25	430	38	768	4	1,156	47
Intermediate zone												
8. Single family, individual services[c]	1,888	91	2,884	73	d	d	837	81	18,786	95+	2,468	72
9. Single family, shared services[e]	1,826	91	2,795	72	d	d	760	78	18,660	95+	2,174	69
10. Single family, basic services[f]	1,765	91	2,706	71	d	d	682	73	18,534	95+	1,880	66
11. Multifamily, individual services	876	76	1,512	50	1,850	45	669	72	4,685	72	1,958	67
12. Multifamily, shared services	762	72	1,310	42	1,684	35	559	63	4,479	70	1,618	61
13. Multifamily, basic services	648	55	1,107	36	1,518	30	448	44	4,272	69	1,278	52

City center

14. Single family, individual services[c]	2,263	95+	10,234	95+	d	d	1,100	88	256,438	95+	18,930	95+
15. Single family, shared services[e]	2,201	95+	10,145	95+	d	d	1,023	87	256,312	95+	18,636	95+
16. Single family, basic services[f]	2,140	95+	10,056	95+	d	d	945	82	256,186	95+	18,342	95+
17. Multifamily, individual services	951	79	2,982	74	12,485	95+	722	75	52,220	95+	5,250	90
18. Multifamily, shared services	837	75	2,780	72	12,319	95+	612	68	52,014	95+	4,910	89
19. Multifamily, basic services	723	70	2,577	70	12,153	95+	501	63	51,807	95+	4,570	87

a. Based on repayment period of twenty-five years, 10 percent interest, no down payment, and 15 percent of household income devoted to housing. Multifamily housing units have 20 square meters of livable space and 15 square meters share of land in a four-story building.

b. Peripheral and intermediate land prices are those prevailing at existing low-cost housing estates; city center land prices are estimates for areas adjacent to the city center.

c. Single-family detached housing unit with 20 square meters of livable space and 75 square meters of land. Services include individual water, toilet, and kitchen.

d. No single-family units built.

e. Communal water supply, sewerage, and other services; site preparation and lighting.

f. Single family: centrally located water and pit latrines plus minimal security lighting and site preparation; multifamily: greater sharing of facilities.

Source: Calculated from Table A17 through A21 in the statistical appendix.

quired monthly payments on the dwelling—is given in appendix Table A22. The results suggest that the lowest 20 percent of families can afford housing at intermediate locations only with subsidies ranging from 23 percent to 93 percent of their monthly housing payments. At these locations, reductions in service levels make little difference. At the periphery, however, a reduction from individual to basic services can eliminate the need for subsidy, even for the poorest 10 percent of families in Mexico City (single-family and multifamily housing) and in Bogotá (single-family housing).

In addition to land costs, changes in service levels can affect the affordability of dwellings. A reduction from single-family individual to basic services at peripheral locations could reach an additional 6 percent of households in Bogotá, 7 percent in Ahmedabad, 8 percent in Mexico City, 9 percent in Madras, and 14 percent in Nairobi. At intermediate locations the calculated cost savings are generally smaller.

The decline in land price as distance from the city center increases affects the choice of dwelling type for the poor in two other important ways. First, it heavily influences the degree to which land and services can substitute for each other. If the decline is steep, as in Mexico City and Bogotá, a reduction in service levels from individual to basic would have little impact at an intermediate location. Thus, although only 17 percent of single-family households in Bogotá could not afford a peripheral dwelling with individual services, 73 percent would not be served in the intermediate zone. Even with basic services this figure can be reduced only to 71 percent. In Nairobi, in which construction costs are high[3] and the relative influence of land cost is less, the situation is quite different. The rise in land price from peripheral to intermediate locations just offsets the fall in land servicing and construction costs if basic services are introduced, and the same percent of families could pay for newly constructed housing. In Madras, on the other hand, more people could be reached at intermediate zones with basic services than at the periphery with individual services.

Second, declines in land price may be counterbalanced by higher costs of multistory construction. As distance outward from the city center increases, the price of land falls to a point at which single-family dwellings are cheaper than multifamily dwellings. In Bogotá single-family dwellings are cheaper at the periphery, whereas multifamily structures are cheaper in intermediate zones. In Mexico City rising land cost clearly invites economizing on land by building upward in intermediate areas. At the periphery of Mexico City the costs of single-family and multifamily structures are about the same.

3. See E. J. Wells and E. R. Rado, *Constraints and Costs in the Kenya Building Industry* (Nairobi: University College, November 1968).

The data in Table 5.7 also show that, in low-income cities such as Ahmedabad and Madras, even the lowest-cost solution at these standards would not reach the bottom 40 percent of the urban population. Other measures would be necessary. One such measure worth considering in some situations is a reduction in livable space per household, perhaps from 20 to 10 square meters (Table 5.8). This standard, combined with various dwelling types and service levels, could reach substantially more households in Ahmedabad, Madras, and Nairobi, though the impact is less marked for Bogotá and Mexico City. This result could then be compared with the cost and desirability of a larger area at similar locations provided under a sites-and-services scheme. Another measure, particularly important when peripheral locations deprive many families of access to jobs and services, is higher residential densities at intermediate locations. As suggested by Table 5.9, high-density single-family construction is a potentially feasible way to house the poor—for example, in Madras—provided appropriate standards are adopted. In other cities such as Bogotá row houses and other dense construction could reach about the same proportion at intermediate zones as detached single-family houses on larger lots at the periphery. In still other cities this type of construction would be less effective, and a multistory solution would be indicated.

Administrative and maintenance costs are included for the Hong Kong examples, which are based on actual, full-cost experience. Where ownership is not an option in multistory housing, the management costs of public housing may be important. Therefore, a cost increase of one-third to account for these costs, as well as for interest during construction and possible delinquencies or defaults in rental payments, was calculated. If costs were one-third higher, the above results for Mexico City and Bogotá would change little. For multifamily dwellings with basic services at the periphery, for example, 7 percent of Mexico City families would not be served, compared with 4 percent without the increase; 23 percent would not be reached in Bogotá, as compared with 15 percent without the increase. But in low-income cities with relatively flat income distributions, such as Ahmedabad and Madras, substantially fewer people could afford the cheapest dwelling. In Ahmedabad 56 percent would not be served with a one-third cost increase, compared with 41 percent without the increase, and in Madras, 62 percent, compared with 38 percent, could not afford housing of this type. In such cities the wisdom of housing solutions emphasizing direct construction would therefore be questionable, and other programs, especially sites and services and squatter upgrading, would be needed to reach poor families.

Other factors, of course, may either increase or reduce the propor-

Table 5.8. Estimated Percentage of Population Unable to Afford Housing of Various Space Standards at Peripheral Locations, by Type of Housing, Selected Cities

Type of housing[a]	Ahmedabad		Bogotá		Madras		Mexico City		Nairobi	
	20 square meters	10 square meters	20 square meters	10 square meters	20 square meters	10 square meters	20 square meters	10 square meters	20 square meters	10 square meters
Single family, individual services	58	30	17	9	77	61	14	5	66	39
Single family, basic services	51	22	11	6	68	39	6	3	52	24
Multifamily, individual services	64	31	36	10	70	29	12	2	65	33
Multifamily, basic services	41	14	15	3	38	10	4	1	47	18

a. Based on repayment period of twenty-five years, 10 percent interest, no down payment, and 15 percent of household income devoted to housing. Single family = single-family detached housing unit with 20 square meters of livable space and 75 square meters of land. Individual services = individual water, toilet, and kitchen. Basic services = for single family, centrally located water and pit latrines plus minimal security lighting and site preparation; for multifamily, greater sharing of facilities. Multifamily = multifamily housing unit with 20 square meters of livable space and 15 square meters share of land in a four-story building.

Source: Calculated from Tables A17 through A21 in the statistical appendix.

Table 5.9. Percentage of Population not Served by Peripheral and Higher-Density Alternatives in Intermediate Zones, Single-Family Dwellings, Selected Cities

		At intermediate locations		
City	At the periphery	Dwellings similar to those at periphery[a]	Smaller dwellings[b]	Higher-density construction[c]
Ahmedabad	58	91	77	64
Bogotá	17	73	47	21
Madras	77	81	27	14
Mexico City	14	95+	93	74
Nairobi	66	72	49	40

a. Single-family detached dwelling; individual water, toilet, and kitchen; 20 square meters of livable space on a 75–square-meter plot.
b. 10 square meters of livable space on a 37.5–square-meter plot.
c. 10 square meters of livable space on a 20–square-meter plot.
Source: Calculated from Tables A17 through A21 in the statistical appendix.

tion of families able to afford the housing solutions described. Families may choose to spend 20 percent rather than 15 percent of their income on housing; this has the same effect on the affordability of housing as a cost reduction of one-third. An increase in the interest rate from 10 to 15 percent, on the other hand, would more than offset this rise in the proportion of income spent on housing.

The preceding illustrations, it must be stressed, should not be interpreted as being indicative of where and how the poor should live within cities. Nor do they establish an optimal residential density or suggest circumstances in which higher densities are required. Present information about the social costs imposed by lack of access to employment opportunities is too limited to permit a more careful weighing of the tradeoffs between peripheral and more central locations. Sites-and-services and squatter-upgrading programs, which stress low space standards and high proportions of self-help construction, hold the most promise of reaching the poor in many instances. Even if the full costs were known, the results would be no more than indicative of what could be accomplished in a variety of political and sociological contexts. If the solutions are to be socially successful, the perceived private costs of the housing solutions proposed will have to be weighed against those of squatting and other options open to low-income families. The examples are intended merely to illustrate, first, ways in which markets operate currently with distortions in demand and supply, and, second, the levers available to policymakers to stimulate low-cost housing production and to increase the participation of the poor in urban housing markets.

Six

Market Imperfections

THE FAILURE OF MARKET FORCES to respond with greater supplies of housing at prices that will meet effective demand is traceable in part to imperfections in housing markets. The urban housing market can be defined in a framework of supply and demand. The effective demand for housing in static terms is a function of income levels and the price of housing and other goods. It is made up of consumption expenditure by families at all income levels, government expenditure on housing (for example, to house government employees), and the demand for structures as assets in investment portfolios, usually exercised by the financial sector. Over time, demand is determined by increases in family income, changes in the distribution of income, and the rate of household formation, which in turn depends upon population growth and size of households. Rich and poor alike demand housing for its quality and location and exercise preferences for housing services compared with other consumer purchases. As incomes rise and basic housing needs are satisfied, a smaller proportion of income may be devoted to housing.

The supply of housing services depends upon the amount of productive resources—land, labor, capital, and management—made available for expansion and maintenance of the urban housing stock. On the supply side the housing market includes all factors of production directly involved in the construction and maintenance of housing, as well as in the provision of management, marketing, finance, insurance, and related services. The size of the housing stock changes only slowly because housing is a relatively durable good. Annual increases in dwelling units—new construction plus renovation of existing units—typically constitute only about 1 to 3 percent of the existing housing stock. Consequently, the supply of housing is also relatively inelastic.

In the face of large increases in the formation of urban households and the progression of income levels, shifts in demand tend to outstrip the response of suppliers. In the market rationing process, the relatively inelastic supply of housing is allocated to the highest bidder. Low-income households are able to purchase only what higher-income households do not want.

Supply response is further constrained by the high transport costs of building materials and the fixed location of dwellings, factors that tend to make housing markets local rather than national in scope.[1] A shortage of housing in city A cannot be met by expanding production in city B and exporting the surplus. Although some factors of production, particularly labor and finance, are fairly mobile, they are combined in a manner reflecting the unique size and contours of one site in one city. The completed dwelling then embodies sunk costs—a stock of irretrievable capital that society has no choice (short of demolition or abandonment) but to try to use to maximum advantage.

This situation implicitly assumes, first, that markets work perfectly; second, that full information (or at least equal cost information) is available to all; third, that no collusion takes place among buyers and sellers; and, fourth, that institutional and regulatory constraints are absent. But housing markets, like many others, are replete with imperfections that prevent demand from being exercised or supply from responding to the desired extent. Housing becomes more scarce and thus more costly. By raising the cost of housing to all, the process of delivering housing services to the poor is made more difficult. More families than necessary find themselves unable to afford suitable housing, and low-income groups are least able to compete for the scarce supply.

In these situations households are forced to lower their expectations and settle for lower-quality accommodation—structurally, spatially, and locationally—than otherwise would be necessary. An intricate pattern of settlement arises because of the pressures on the housing stock and the fact that housing can be a source of income to its owner. Aside from the two common forms of tenure—owner and renter accommodation—found (in different proportions) everywhere, there are shared and subrented dwellings. Rental payments can be horizontal—that is,

1. See Lionel Needleman, *The Economics of Housing* (London: Staples Press, 1965), pp. 105–06.

to other low-income families—or vertical—to middle- and high-income landlords. This diversity of tenure arrangements may include the sharing and renting out of squatter huts. At each step of renting out and sharing space, income opportunities are exploited in a tight housing market.

Certain attributes of housing are inherent in all housing markets rather than being imperfections whose elimination could be brought about through public policy. The durability of housing, for example, produces different rates of construction based on each family's expected streams of benefits and costs from housing in the future—all of which may differ from the rate at which society perceives benefits and costs. Externalities, particularly the quality of the neighborhood environment, affect household decisions to construct or improve housing. Finally, since housing is spatially fixed, the cost of changing dwellings or moving the dwelling itself may be high.[2] These features distinguish the housing market from others and help determine the allocation of housing resources among different income groups.

True imperfections in housing markets can be classified broadly as institutional or economic in nature. The institutional constraints generally arise from legal barriers and administrative controls that have been erected to protect specific groups or interests. Modification of these constraints improves the operation of housing markets. The economic imperfections, on the other hand, are less straightforward. In this case, basic economic relations in the production of housing or in measuring its worth give rise to fundamental problems within the mechanism of market allocation.

Institutional constraints

Several types of administrative controls effectively reduce the flow of resources into the housing sector. Zoning, for example, is often used to prevent specific land parcels from being allocated to the highest bidder, either by imposing limited categories of use or by restricting unit density. Building codes, which are ostensibly designed to protect the consumer who has limited ability to judge quality of structures, often protect suppliers of outmoded materials or favored building trades. The benefits of newer, less expensive materials and more com-

2. These costs explain why only the relatively expensive parts of a house, such as the roof and windows, may go with a squatter family to a new location, while the mud and thatch shells remain, to erode away. See Mission d'Urbanisme, *Kinshasa: Plan Local d'Amenagement* (Kinshasa: 1965).

petitive labor markets are thereby denied the consumer. Although the impact of institutional rigidities of this kind on housing supply has not been analyzed, evidence for advanced countries suggests that construction costs are unnecessarily increased by the restrictive nature of local building codes.[3] In Bogotá regulations have required that high-rise construction take place on a street or corner, not in the interior of a block. The potential saving in land costs by building upwards may thus be mitigated by the fact that the construction must occur on higher-priced land.

Minimum wage legislation and unionization have also been blamed for limiting the flow of labor into the housing sector and for raising unit construction costs. Unionization may have been a factor contributing to the greater increase in wages than in materials costs in recent years in the Mexican housing industry.[4] This effect may be especially significant in countries in which labor is prevented from working at the value of its marginal product and is therefore underused.

Rent controls similarly distort the market by inhibiting expansion and maintenance of the housing stock. Even though rent control may bring about lower rents on controlled buildings, all other poor families are forced to compete for uncontrolled housing similar in quality but with higher rental payments.[5] In Mexico City control of rents on central city tenements has led to large differences in rents for similar accommodations and to deterioration of the controlled structures.[6] Owners of controlled housing have less incentive to maintain or rehabilitate their properties, and builders are equally loath to expand their activities in a market in which price control is added to other public regulations. Thus, on both counts, the housing stock undergoes a relative reduction over time. Furthermore, poor families who succeed in obtaining controlled housing are not necessarily better off in the long run. They may pay more in maintenance than they save in rent. Mobil-

---

3. See U.S. Advisory Commission on Intergovernmental Relations, *Building Codes: A Program for Intergovernmental Reform*, report no. 28 (Washington, D.C.: Government Printing Office, 1966).

4. See, for example, C. Araud, G. Boon, V. Urquidi, and W. P. Strassmann, *Studies on Employment in the Mexican Housing Industry* (Paris: Organization for Economic Cooperation and Development, 1973).

5. On the economic effects of rent control, see Jerome Rothenberg, *Economic Evaluation of Urban Renewal* (Washington, D.C.: Brookings Institution, 1967); and Jorgen H. Gelting, "On the Economic Effects of Rent Control in Denmark," in Adela Adam Nevitt (ed.), *Economic Problems of Housing* (New York: Macmillan, 1967), pp. 85–91.

6. John F. C. Turner and Tomasz Sudra, "Housing Needs and Users' Priorities" (Washington, D.C.: World Bank, 1974; processed).

ity is also lessened, since families in controlled housing are much less free to move in response to changes in employment locations.

The institutional arrangements governing housing finance may also inhibit the mobilization of savings or distort its allocation. Interest rate ceilings on mortgages and deposits in mortgage lending institutions limit the flow of financial resources into the housing sector, particularly during periods of high interest rates, sometimes preventing the housing industry from competing for scarce funds. Collateral requirements may weigh more heavily on the poor, whose only form of collateral may be in human rather than physical capital. Low-income households may also have to pay interest rates that bear no clear relation to risk on their borrowings and to repay loans over short periods of time. Under some arrangements the term of mortgages is limited to fifteen years or less, which hampers the ability of poor families to repay. These circumstances strongly reinforce the tendency for the supply of new housing to go first and foremost to middle- and upper-income families, because the market allocates to these income groups the limited supply of institutionalized savings that is not used for such other purposes as industrial investment.

The obtaining of clear tenure to land increases the cost of participation in real estate markets, especially for low-income households who are least able to follow the appropriate registration procedures. Expensive legal and brokerage assistance is generally needed to secure land. A sorting out of conflicting ownership claims and provision of assistance in title registration can help remove a disincentive to investment in improvements on land resulting from uncertainties of this kind.

Poor households are less likely than others to be able to evade such institutional barriers. Through personal connections, high-income families can often sidestep snags and delays in obtaining permission to build, whereas the poor must wait in line for the necessary permits or—if they do build illegally—must live in fear of eviction. Developers of high-cost housing often know of planning decisions in advance. They may then buy land before its price rises steeply or may acquire alternative sites. Information on building techniques is more readily available to those who can hire workers with specialized skills than to those who must learn informally on their own.

Economic imperfections

With economic imperfections, the flow of resources into the housing sector is constrained by, for example, the availability of infrastructure needed to service housing. Indivisibilities in the supply of infrastructure—productive factors suppliable economically only in fixed (usually minimum) amounts—cause the production of housing to be uneven and often badly coordinated. Pricing and management rules of public utilities may also unnecessarily restrict the access of the poor to public services at reasonable cost. High installation charges, for example, may be incompatible with income levels of the poor. Rules of financial management restrict overall supply. Such difficulties are compounded when boundaries of land parcels need to be adjusted to harmonize with street contours. On other occasions tiny parcels must be amalgamated to form units of viable size. Because of the prohibitively high transaction costs of grouping the demands of many people, each with small holdings, this process is difficult for the poor. Rich landowners, on the other hand, can and do band together to undertake many kinds of land assembly schemes.

Transaction and information costs also affect the degree to which changes in prices and rentals of dwellings can lead to their use by different income groups. Since housing shortages exist at all income levels, the unsatisfied demand at any level normally adds to the effective demand at the next lower level. But, if high income groups demand new housing because of wear and tear on existing high-quality structures, obsolescence, or changes in tastes, the resulting new construction may relieve some pressure on the demand for existing dwellings and cause them to fall in value. The most dilapidated structures will no longer be needed and may be abandoned. Owners of similar housing would then be forced to lower rents to remain competitive. These forces may bring housing at each successive income level within the reach of groups that previously could not afford it.

Scattered evidence suggests, however, that this filtering process does not contribute greatly to improving housing conditions for the poor. In squatter areas information about housing in other parts of the city is typically scarce.[7] Search costs and other outlays of money and time contribute to a high cost of moving and limit the type of family mobility customary in high-income countries. Craftsmen, shopkeepers, and small traders have often built up a network of customers and staked out a territory that they are loath to give up. Many moves among low-income families appear to have more to do with the dilapidated state of their present house than with the emergence of better condi-

7. See Iris Kapil and Hasan Gencaga, "Urbanization and Modernization in Turkey," Discussion Paper no. 10 (Ankara, Turkey: U.S. Agency for International Development, July 1972), especially p. 20.

tions in other neighborhoods.[8] Filtering may also lead to reduced maintenance of rental dwellings by landlords, leaving poor families no better off.

Whether imperfections in the housing market specifically or in the economy generally are more responsible for raising the cost of housing can be ascertained by comparing rates of return earned from housing development with those in other sectors. Available information indicates that investment in squatter housing can be enormously profitable. In many developing countries poor people pay rents that yield returns on capital of from 30 to 100 percent a year.[9] When underinvestment in housing is this severe, efforts to reduce market imperfections in the housing sector could achieve substantial results.

The time needed to bring about reductions in imperfections, however, should not be underestimated. Realistically, programs to assist dwelling construction for low-income families, whether or not they can afford market housing, will take decades to design, staff, and put into practice. In the meantime, urbanization will continue at a high rate. For these reasons a much larger proportion than the lowest 10 to 20 percent of households will not be able to pay the economic cost of housing in the near future. Action to supplement market forces is required if better housing is to be provided for them.

Subsidies and market interdependence

Subsidies have been used in many countries, both developing and developed, as a tool of public policy to provide housing for low-income households unable to afford housing in the market. In the United States direct subsidies to low-income households amounted to some US$3.4 billion in 1970. An additional US$5.4 billion of subsidies was

8. Ibid. For a discussion of filtering in U.S. housing markets, see Ira Lowry, "Filtering and Housing Standards: A Conceptual Analysis," *Land Economics*, vol. 36 (November 1960), pp. 362–70; William G. Grigsby, *Housing Markets and Public Policy* (Philadelphia: University of Pennsylvania Press, 1963), pp. 84–130; Wallace F. Smith, *Housing: The Social and Economic Elements* (Berkeley, Calif.: University of California Press, 1970), pp. 357–64; and John B. Lansing, Charles Wade Clifton, and James N. Morgan, *New Homes and Poor People: A Study of Chains of Moves* (Ann Arbor, Mich.: Institute for Social Research, University of Michigan, 1969). The last study demonstrated that for every 1,000 homes constructed, 3,545 changes of residence occurred, but less than 10 percent of this total were by poor families.

9. John E. Murphy, *Shelter Program Objectives* (Washington, D.C.: U.S. Agency for International Development, October 1974), p. 2.

provided to households with higher incomes, in the form of mortgage interest and property tax deductions from taxable personal income.[10]

A principal objective of a subsidy scheme is to alter the composition of economic activity, through changes in the relative prices of subsidized and unsubsidized goods and services. Among the economic justifications offered for subsidies are, first, the assumed inability of producers and consumers to bring about an optimal allocation of resources, and, second, price and supply rigidities deriving from regulations, legislative enactments, and abuse of market power. The argument holds that these inefficiencies may be severe enough in some cases that government intervention can make some persons better off without making others worse off. Subsidies might be used to help mitigate the effects of the market imperfections discussed above so as to improve the workings of housing markets.

Moreover, subsidies have also been justified as a means of redistributing income. As such, they must compete with subsidies for education, health, nutrition, and other socioeconomic sectors. Total economic output may be considered improperly allocated if the distribution of goods and services does not accord with society's ethical values. The economic significance of housing and its importance in urban spatial form make it a prime candidate in many instances for consideration for subsidy. Yet if care is not taken in their selection and application, housing subsidies can accrue to middle- or even high-income families, thereby depriving the poor of needed resources. In this situation income redistribution is difficult, since constraints on these resources in the cities of developing countries make it impossible to subsidize housing broadly or continuously. This is one example of how actions at one level of the housing market will have repercussions on the entire market and of why a comprehensive set of policy measures is called for to deal with the market as a whole.

Although housing must satisfy demands by consumers having different income levels and varied preferences, the housing market consists of interdependent parts. Attempts to correct market imperfections by introducing a program at one level will spread through the rest of the housing market. Only by understanding how the entire market functions will it be possible to predict the consequences of various programs and to avoid unintended results. For example, it is common to see sites-and-services projects that are designed for low-income groups be occupied in the end by middle-income groups. The

10. Harrison Wehner, *Sections 235 and 236: An Economic Evaluation of HUD's Principal Housing Subsidy Programs* (Washington, D.C.: American Enterprise Institute for Public Policy Research, 1973), p. 17.

reason is that the housing demands of the middle-income group are also not met by the market, and that the purchasing power and political influence of the relatively affluent are more effective than those of the lower-income groups. In these instances the generally welcome addition to the housing stock provides an unwanted conduit for the trickling-up of resources meant for the poor—which produces unintended redistribution effects and poses a difficult challenge for public policy.

Seven

Housing Policy Options

SOME HIGH-INCOME COUNTRIES have found housing—and more generally urban development—difficult to organize efficiently and equitably, even though they have not had to deal with the same explosive city growth as developing countries. It is therefore not surprising that most developing countries, with low incomes and limited resources, find housing a nearly intractable policy area.

Several developed and some developing countries have been able, however, to provide the bulk of their populations with housing that is economic and yet meets reasonable welfare requirements, and sites-and-services and squatter-upgrading programs are often the best way to provide housing and services the poor can afford in many low-income countries. Suitably designed, multifamily dwellings can add to the options available to poor families and increase opportunities for improving the spatial layout of cities, particularly for the higher-income developing countries. The interaction between land availability and servicing and the provision of housing makes a high degree of government involvement inevitable, even if most of the housing market remains in the hands of private enterprise.

Developing countries have a wide range of models on which to draw in designing housing policy. More to the point, in most countries improvement in policy can contribute substantially to better housing without a major commitment of additional resources. Drawing on the positive experiences of several countries, notably Hong Kong and Singapore, this chapter outlines the elements of a housing policy in

91

which public action is regarded as complementary to private initiative. In this way, the less successful experiences with land policy, building standards, and other aspects of housing supply studied in previous chapters are contrasted with programs that stand a much better chance of reaching low-income families.

The policy framework

Since housing market activities take place within the general framework of national and urban development, the context within which policies are drawn up and applied has important implications for both supply and demand factors influencing housing. Through their effects on a country's international price competitiveness, exchange, foreign trade, and other commercial policies have important effects on the cost of developing urban land, constructing dwellings, and providing urban services. Many construction materials enjoy a large degree of natural protection because of their weight and bulk, but in some countries they also are protected by a variety of trade policies. Such tendencies are sometimes worsened by licensing and other procedures that limit competitiveness among producers. Thus, construction materials tend to be costly, particularly in small countries with a relatively low level of industrial development that have chosen a highly protectionist policy, and there is little adaptation of new construction materials to local needs. Countries may, of course, opt for a protectionist policy but offset its negative effects by stimulating internal competitiveness. Such competitiveness is relatively easy to organize in large countries, but since many construction-related industries have no significant economies of scale, it is also feasible even in relatively small countries. In India, in spite of high protection, there is a great deal of internal competitiveness in the production of construction materials. Direct government encouragement of the development of new construction materials has led to the availability of the lowest-priced building materials and construction methods in the world. Countries with open economies such as Hong Kong and Singapore have also benefited from the cheapness of their construction materials.

Monetary policy is an important factor in the availability of housing finance. The lack of a grass-roots type of mortgage institution—often the consequence of inappropriate interest rate structures—creates distortions in savings patterns that may discriminate against housing. Only a long-term improvement in monetary and capital market policy can redress such a situation. Countries with chronic inflation generally must resort to almost continuous and severe credit rationing. This limits the role of credit in bringing unused or underused resources into productiveness by stimulating the housing market—a limitation that is particularly unfortunate during a downswing in the economic cycle.

Fiscal policy also is critical to a country's ability to mobilize its resources for growth and an equitable distribution of income. Poorly conceived or administered fiscal policy, moreover, is often a principal cause of long-run inflationary tendencies. Budgetary shortages are often reflected most acutely in reduced expenditure on sectors such as housing.

Labor policy can hinder the development of housing. Unduly rigid skill requirements are sometimes combined with restrictive entry conditions into building trades. Far from protecting the rights of the workers, such restrictions limit housing construction and thereby reduce employment below the level that could be sustained with more liberal policies. In some countries onerous licensing and inappropriate inspection procedures create monopolistic and oligopolistic privileges for construction firms, which also may inhibit housing construction.

Much of the imperfection of housing markets is thus derived from a country's overall economic policy framework. All such policies influence the spatial dimensions of national housing programs in urban areas of different sizes. It is not possible to adopt strict criteria as to the size of city that best conforms to a given set of national development policies. Rather, a range of city sizes can be compatible with orderly urban growth.[1] Countries with a poorly conceived economic policy cannot expect to deal effectively with their housing problems. In addition, the economic and welfare characteristics of housing and associated urban development also lead most countries toward a relatively high direct government involvement in these areas.

Because important components of the housing package—access roads, utilities, and, to some degree, transport—are natural monopolies, they require public ownership or regulation if supply is to be responsive and excessive monopoly profits are to be controlled. Historically, public utility institutions and controls have usually developed separately for water and sewerage, electricity, and transport and other communications, and most countries are now faced by an extremely complex, often inconsistent regulatory framework for these services.

1. See Irving Hoch, "Income and City Size," in Gordon C. Cameron and Lowdon Wingo (eds.), *Cities, Regions and Public Policy* (Edinburgh: Oliver and Boyd, 1973), pp. 125–54; George S. Tolley, "Economic Policy Toward City Bigness," *Proceedings of Inter-University Committee on Urban Economics* (1969); and Norman H. Lithwick and Gilles Paquet, "Urban Growth and Regional Contagion," in *Urban Studies: A Canadian Perspective* (Toronto: Methuen, 1968).

The interdependent nature of these monopolies makes their control difficult but no less necessary.

The existence of external costs and benefits also leads to a need for public intervention. Some externalities such as pollution and road congestion are clear examples of unintended harmful effects; there is usually little objection to control of them by public authorities. On the other hand, land development as urbanization proceeds gives rise to benefits whose consequences are less clear. Unless special efforts are made to appropriate some of these benefits for social use, the increases in value will accrue to those individuals fortunate enough to be landowners. Such a situation may result in more investment in land than is felt to be socially desirable and may also encourage clearance of squatter areas.

The social implications of housing provide another reason for government intervention. Such intervention may be designed to mitigate the effects of market imperfections (particularly in land) that are too difficult to attack directly but that discriminate particularly against the poor and reduce their productivity. Housing subsidies, for example, may be justified on grounds of increasing productivity or as a means of redistributing income to increase the welfare of the very poor.

An effective housing policy requires not only sound strategy but also effective administration. The experience of most cities in developing countries suggests that existing approaches do not give enough weight to the need for efficient institutions with a focus on unique local conditions. Emphasis must be given to the fostering of institutions capable of formulating and executing urban development plans and, within them, housing programs.

Policy instruments

The range of instruments available for carrying out housing strategies and policies is considerable. Most instruments have a number of effects, some of them not always anticipated, but sufficient experience has by now been accumulated to enable some general judgments to be made about the value of particular instruments and their most appropriate use.

Zoning

A potentially valuable instrument of urban and housing policy, zoning is important in protecting an aesthetically pleasing residential environment, grouping commercial and other activities in an efficient manner, and segregating activities that interfere with one another. It must, however, be used in a dynamic context, with an appreciation of the realities of poverty in the present, as well as of future development goals. For example, the inappropriate application of zoning regulations suited to developed countries may exclude the poor from residence near industrial, commercial, and high-income residential zones that provide their greatest opportunities for earning income. At worst, misapplication of zoning concepts leads to clearance of slum and squatter housing, which undermines employment opportunities at the same time that it destroys housing. Properly used, zoning can help to ensure an ample supply of urban land as a city expands—and can do so in such a way that the gains are at least shared, if not largely captured, by the public purse on behalf of society. Hong Kong and Singapore have been able to combine zoning measures with land development, housing construction, and the provision of land for industry with the result that costs have been minimized, the housing industry has been stimulated, and workers have been provided access to employment either nearby or through cheap and convenient transport. Zoning regulations in many other countries, however, have imposed heavy transport costs on low-income families and sometimes even deprived them of job access by requiring separation of residential from industrial and commercial areas.

Controls on building standards

Appropriate building standards can also do much to create a safe and pleasant environment. They may be required to prevent or limit the consequences of fires, earthquakes, floods, and similar disasters. Misconceived, however, they can contribute to depressing the living standards of the poor. If such regulations are inappropriate and set standards too high for existing income levels, their primary effect will be to reduce the amount of housing that is available at prices the poor can afford. Bamboo, thatch, and other traditional materials are sometimes prohibited by building standard controls, although other appropriate measures could avoid the fire hazards that these materials are alleged to create. Under inappropriate regulations, the poor will often be driven to bribery in order to retain or construct housing classified as "substandard."

Land management

The availability of low-cost, serviced land that is accessible to employment and other services has been a major element in the most successful housing programs. But the strongly rising demand for land that accompanies population growth and household formation often makes the provision of such land difficult. Moreover, imperfections such as those mentioned earlier normally hamper the operation of private land markets. In these instances public measures are often taken to control the use of private land and to increase the provision of serviced sites.

Land tenure. In many countries land ownership is at least as complex and as inequitably distributed in urban as in rural areas. Introducing an element of equity into urban land ownership by giving squatters security of tenure is an urgent policy issue in most cities in developing countries—one with high income returns, in retained and improved housing stock and in access to earning opportunities. The sorting out of ownership claims in peripheral areas, before tenure problems arise, is equally important.

Land resumption and purchase. To solve housing and associated urban development problems equitably, most developed countries have found it necessary to redefine land property rights and to purchase urban land. Some developing countries own public land that can be used for such purposes directly; alternatively, the funds from its sale may be used to purchase other, perhaps more useful, land. Still others face the formidable problem of creating a land reserve. For the most part, the purchase of land within existing city limits is costly, but peripheral land generally can be purchased ahead of use at low cost. Because present owners of such land are often farmers using the land productively, a variety of deferred payment schemes can be used to purchase it while temporarily retaining its present use.

Even in such circumstances, land purchase is difficult in practice because of the enormous windfalls that can be obtained by officials or private individuals through information leaks and speculation. The potential gains for urban development are so great, however, that the risks are worth taking. Iran, for example, has combined the imposition of zoning with the purchase of urban parcels in advance of need. With good management, the increasing value of serviced land can be appropriated for social use and can help finance the cost of urban development over time.

Land development. Several countries have sought to stimulate housing by increasing the supply of serviced land. Hong Kong and Singapore have both been active in this respect. In Chile the Corporación de la Vivienda developed about four times more land from agricultural to urban use than all private interests combined in the decade before 1968.[2] Lebanon permits private development of urban

2. Robert N. Merrill, *An Evaluation of Chile's Housing Program: Problems and Prospects* (M.A. thesis, Cornell University, June 1968), p. 77.

land according to publicly approved plans and with the participation of the state and municipalities as shareholders. Programs of this kind, common in France, have also been adopted in several French-speaking countries, particularly in West Africa. Other examples can be cited: in Nairobi ownership of public land is regulated by legislation that involves a variety of holdings including complete freehold and grants of long- and short-term leases. As in many other cities throughout the world, however, the municipal government has rarely exercised these powers, with the result that public freehold land is rapidly used up.

Land development may be undertaken by a combination of public and private means. In an increasingly popular method—used in Malaysia, Korea, Colombia (where it is known as "valorization"), Sri Lanka, and Taiwan—public land development agencies open land for residential construction; associations of landowners may then undertake projects involving amalgamation of parcels and installation of public facilities on sites. In Korea cities participate directly in reshaping rural properties into a pattern of urban streets, schools, and parks, with plots for private construction. These "land readjustment" schemes have been responsible for the development of large sections of Seoul and other principal cities. The Mexican government has been actively involved in the acquisition of privately owned land for urban residential reserves, which are then leased to private developers on a long-term basis. Land development schemes in many cases include commercial and industrial centers as well as residential facilities. Governments in some countries have supplemented these programs by encouraging employers to provide housing for their workers, either through loan guarantees or by direct construction. Others have avoided this path on the premise that housing tied to jobs puts the worker at a disadvantage.

Taxes on land. Major instruments of policy, particularly in combination with other land-planning measures, are land taxes and user charges, which can capture for social use some of the gains, or "betterment" values, accruing to land and housing owners in urban areas. In most countries land taxes usually constitute a minor part of the fiscal system but can be improved substantially through reforms in assessment and collection procedures. Nor must the gains be limited to increased local and national revenue. More adequate taxation, if it were combined with special taxes or higher rates for unimproved land, could reduce incentives to hold land for speculative purposes. Taiwan combines a land value tax with a tax on land price increments at the time of sale. Korea's 50 percent increment tax was designed to control land speculation. Betterment taxation is also used in Lebanon, Peru,

Colombia, Uruguay, and elsewhere. In practice, an inability to keep assessments up to date and the granting of exemptions—often politically motivated—can severely constrain the effectiveness of land tax measures. Nevertheless, there is a growing recognition of the advantages of taxes on urban land as effective policy instruments.[3]

Rent controls and subsidies

The use of rent controls to prevent private individuals from capturing socially caused gains and to mitigate the imperfections of housing markets has a long and unsuccessful history in developed as well as developing countries. Rent controls have been effective only for limited periods of strong social cohesion, as during wartime, and when applied in combination with strict controls on other incomes and prices. Applied over longer periods, rent controls have led in most countries to illegal rationing systems by which payments such as "key money" become a substitute for proper rents. The poor may be driven out of much of the controlled housing. Because rent controls force legal returns on housing that are below market levels, they lead to disinvestment and the deterioration of housing through lack of maintenance, as in Mexico City. They also inhibit additions to the housing stock, particularly for private investment in housing. But even if a substantial public housing effort exists or attempts are made to take over controlled properties, heavy subsidies are often necessary. Rent controls also reduce the amount of public funds available from taxation because the illegal payments are not taxed. The housing stock and, consequently, the flow of income do not expand. Attempts to control the prices of public utilities or urban transport have had similar financial repercussions.[4]

Price subsidies for housing, as for associated services, may in some circumstances be a useful instrument for redistributing income. They are feasible in relatively high-income and in some middle-income

3. See Orville F. Grimes, Jr., "Urban Land and Public Policy: Social Appropriation of Betterment," World Bank Staff Working Paper no. 179 (May 1974) and in Paul B. Downing (ed.), *Local Service Pricing and Urban Spatial Structure* (Vancouver, B.C.: University of British Columbia Press, forthcoming); and "Reappraising Urban Land Tax Effectiveness against Policy Goals," in *Urban Systems Research*, Report no. PB-241 120, ed. John W. Dickey and Roy W. R. Muncey (Washington, D.C.: National Technical Information Service, April 1975), pp. 267–80.

4. Such services are typically restricted to middle- and upper–middle-income areas. The poor are seriously disadvantaged, and stocks and services deteriorate. In addition, the location choices of households and businesses may become more restricted.

developing countries to assist the poor. Subsidies, mainly in the form of charging below-market prices for publicly owned land and government loans, have been a feature of successful sites-and-services and low-income housing programs in several countries. For countries rich in natural resources, subsidies for housing and public utilities can be a particularly useful instrument for raising standards of living rapidly. A long tradition of subsidized housing in mining enclaves has distributed at least a small portion of the economic rent accruing to the mine. Housing subsidies are now being used by several oil-rich Middle Eastern countries as a form of income distribution in kind.

The system of cross-subsidization offers a possibility of helping the poor with little or no net fiscal burden falling on the government. Land development is planned so that high-income households pay ground rents that approximate the market value of the land after servicing. Because land is demanded for so many reasons—as a housing site, a means of securing education and jobs, a springboard to greater financial security, and so on—the cost of providing services will almost certainly be less than market value. Payments by high-income households should therefore create a budgetary surplus that can be used to subsidize low-income households. This type of development also has the advantage of bringing together a variety of social groups and of providing easily accessible employment in personal services for the poorer households.

For most developing countries, however, the use of subsidies on a significant scale is severely limited by budgetary considerations. The limited funds available can often be put to more productive uses in other sectors. This situation is most likely to prevail in the poorest countries, in which the low-income groups most need such subsidies. In these countries, however, the failure of housing agencies to recoup the cost of providing housing limits what can be built and often leads to unintended results. Even if the standards of low-income housing are appropriate (as discussed earlier) for the intended income group, and more certainly if they are flexible (as in sites-and-services development) or too high, the limited supply of housing is likely to be raided by higher-income groups, either from the beginning or in later purchases. In either case, it is a wiser policy to move toward standards that the intended beneficiaries can afford: that is, to provide land plots and housing units that they will be able to retain.

The upgrading of squatter settlements by introducing appropriate public utilities and granting security of tenure has a general element of subsidy in it, since squatters are rarely required to pay for the full value of their land in exchange for title. But because not all squatters are among the poorest in a community, such schemes, to prevent raiding and to provide funds for further squatter upgrading, should also require the payment of at least some portion of the actual land value in exchange for the title.

Improvement of financial institutions

A lack or shortage of mortgage funds often retards the provision of sufficient housing. This problem, of course, is not so much one of housing as of development of the financial sector. In most developing countries the building up of a variety of suitable financial intermediaries is the first task—but financial intermediation generally requires reforms in financial markets. Such actions as the freeing of interest rate restrictions, the institution of measures to encourage competition among banks, the ending of inappropriate banking practices, and the promotion of life insurance companies and pension funds will help to increase the availability of long-term credit and, potentially, of financing for an efficient housing sector.

One possible means that combines aspects of financial market development with reaching low- and middle-income groups—particularly in countries with an adequate flow of savings into the housing sector—is to encourage the creation of mechanisms or institutions for mortgage insurance in the public or private sector. Such schemes decrease the down payment required of individual homebuyers by insuring the mortgage lender for a certain percentage of the loan. As a result, mortgage lenders may be able to extend loans that finance 90 percent of the cost of the dwelling, for example, without incurring more risk than if they were financing 70 percent. Thus, homeownership can be made accessible to persons who have a regular income but lack the accumulated wealth required for a down payment of from 30 to 40 percent.

Another means stresses the linking of deposits and loans to changes in the price level in order to protect investors from inflation and to stimulate the flow of resources to the construction sector. The Colombian Savings and Loan Corporations (Corporaciones de Ahorro y Vivienda) have succeeded by this device in rechanneling credit toward construction, but they may also have strained the ability of the financial system to assure adequate flows of funds to other sectors.[5] Israel

5. Albert Goltz and Desmond Lachman, "Monetary Correction and Colombia's Savings and Loan System," *Finance and Development*, vol. 11 (September 1974), pp. 24–26. On recent Brazilian experience, see Walter L. Ness, Jr., "Financial Markets Innovation as a Development Strategy: Initial Results from the Brazilian Experience," *Economic Development and Cultural Change*, vol. 22 (April 1974), pp. 453–73.

has also operated such a system whose coverage has included wages and industrial and agricultural loans in addition to loans for housing.

Removal of the specific hindrances to housing finance would allow housing to compete more effectively with other claimants for long-term institutional finance. Specific measures, and in most cases new institutions, are needed if low-income borrowers are to be able to borrow freely in amounts suited to their needs.

Encouragement of the building materials industry

Developing countries usually have a wide range of renewable local resources, such as timber and agricultural fibers, on which to draw in housing construction, but in most countries their integration into local markets has proceeded slowly. Protection from lower-priced imports may be needed in the early growth stages of some building materials industries, until they become competitive. Timber, for example, can replace more expensive materials for trusses, ceiling joists, and house framing. Shredded rice husks and other agricultural residues can be compressed with earth into adobe bricks or wallboard.

The awarding of government contracts to local entrepreneurs is one initiative which can encourage small-scale industry and labor-intensive techniques in the building materials industries, especially in the production of building equipment, treatment of local building materials to withstand environmental damage, and construction work. Training programs in construction management skills, such as those given by the Kenya National Construction Corporation, can benefit local contractors. Technical assistance can also be provided to help in obtaining short-term credit, sometimes from funds set up especially for this purpose, since small firms may find it difficult to maintain the liquidity necessary for periodic wage payments. Finally, interdisciplinary research on the economic as well as the design aspects of building innovation and construction methods improves the potential for a new technique to penetrate local markets successfully.

Housing and public policy

Public authorities wishing to improve housing conditions for poor families in the context of overall housing development can usually use self-help and formal construction methods in varying proportions. No hard and fast guidelines as to which policies work best can apply in all situations. Where labor is severely underused and incomes are low, sites-and-services programs combined with squatter rehabilitation and upgrading may represent the most effective use of abundant labor and scarce capital. Cooperative housing, which conserves managerial talent while encouraging savings, may also contribute to increasing the housing stock. Formal construction, as argued in earlier chapters, could reach large numbers of the urban poor if appropriately designed—and it can also improve the spatial distribution of people in urban areas. An urban housing policy that uses existing resources efficiently and responds to the capacity to pay of the poor must take these policy options into account, although the blend will vary with the features unique to each city.

Sites-and-services and squatter-upgrading programs

Savings must be accumulated to create additions to the stock of housing capital. The great advantage of the sites-and-services method is that much of the savings needed for this process can be mobilized directly, in kind, rather than indirectly through financial intermediaries. Savings and investment thus occur simultaneously. The future owner has a stake in the process of house construction and is in a position to influence its outcome. Control over the method and speed of construction fosters a sense of self-reliance, just as working with neighbors to install streets and walkways improves community interaction. By phasing construction over a number of years, the owner can improve his dwelling according to his financial capacity. For the community as a whole, the urban development and planning process becomes more manageable.

Enough experience has been accumulated to indicate the elements of a successful sites-and-services policy. Since project participants are often resettled squatters or newly arrived migrants whose former employment may be cut off, an adequate mix of income-earning opportunities for all family members is essential. Middle-income families can outbid the poor for choice sites and finish their houses faster, often by subcontracting large portions of the work. Inappropriately high building standards have also encouraged the poor to sell to more affluent families and resume squatting at other locations. To prevent a sites-and-services project from becoming an entirely middle-income enclave over time, it is usually necessary to provide a spectrum of serviced sites ranging from bare, leveled sites without facilities for the poorest families to larger plots with individual utility connections on which a substantial house may be built.

There is growing concern among policymakers that these projects may result in lower residential densities than are desirable. The land intensiveness of projects has often led to their location on the outskirts of cities, where job access without substantial travel cost may be difficult. The solution to this problem involves not merely a locating of sites next to industrial estates or inducing plants to relocate at the periphery but ensuring that a variety of income-earning opportunities suitable for all family members is within easy reach of the sites. Though the project itself contributes to employment creation and thus to income through value added by self-help and wages paid to hired laborers, such a contribution in the long run can be only marginal.

Since most low-income families are housed by traditional and informal methods, policies that allow for, and support, the upgrading of spontaneous settlements—at standards that may be well below those currently in favor—can strengthen the role of housing in enabling squatters to adapt to urban life. This policy recognizes the general acceptance of modest shelter by the poor, given their low incomes. Such action can stabilize tenure, giving residents a measure of security, and can introduce pathways, standpipes, security lighting, and other minimal facilities. It can help to make the growth of squatter areas more efficient and more socially acceptable.

In Madras and other cities, however, patchwork settlement patterns may already have become too dense to allow installation of services without demolishing some structures. Most upgrading projects usually involve destruction of some dwellings and the need to relocate the displaced families. Therefore, it is desirable in many instances to combine upgrading with sites-and-services programs, so that uprooted families can resettle themselves at roughly comparable costs. Where topography is favorable and there is sufficient vacant land nearby, community facilities may also be added. In plans for the Chetla bustee improvement scheme in Calcutta, for example, extensive areas have been devoted to a shopping center, primary school, park, and playground. At the same time, the new housing is planned to accommodate all persons living and working in the bustee and to allow for additional residents.

Cooperative housing

The sites-and-services and squatter-upgrading methods recognize that low-income families should attempt to meet their housing needs through cooperative efforts. It has long been felt that cooperative housing societies, which pool their resources in building funds often obtained at low interest through public loans, could be an effective method of providing housing for low-income families. But cooperatives in developing countries—patterned loosely after cooperative societies in Denmark, Germany, Sweden, and other high-income countries— have had limited success in reaching low-income families. Their contributions to the overall housing stock have, by and large, been small, and a high proportion of the dwellings has been built to middle-income standards. Managerial and operation problems, the inadequacy of financial resources, and the scarcity of land and building materials have contributed to the difficulties. In India and Bangladesh cooperatives have generally not succeeded in obtaining adequate savings from their members.[6] Collective responsibility for individual debts sometimes leads to default and delinquency in rental payments. These problems are less symptomatic of cooperative housing, however, than of housing market operations in general. The most solid contribution of cooperatives so far to housing the urban poor seems to be in initiating housing solutions tailored to local needs and using private sector resources while at the same time encouraging a sense of community responsibility for finance, public services, and other components of housing that families cannot provide for themselves.

Public housing

Countries that are able to combine the instruments of housing policy available in an effective overall policy framework are ones which strive to minimize market imperfections. In these countries private developers usually perform a positive role, meeting the demand for all but the poorest urban groups, and the spatial layout of growing urban areas is under control. Such countries unfortunately are still few in number; they are also the ones which view housing as an instrument for shaping cities and urban productivity, as well as for contributing to the welfare of low-income households. Public housing experience includes notable successes and resounding failures. Two cities, Hong Kong and Singapore, stand out among the most successful, with some 40 percent of their populations living in public housing units.

The Singapore Housing and Development Board constructed nearly 155,000 self-contained housing units from 1960 to 1972, a higher number of such dwellings completed per capita than any other country. Furthermore, public housing construction has not taken place

6. See Jack Edmonson, *Report on the National Workshop on Low Cost and Cooperative Housing in Bangladesh* (Washington, D.C.: International Cooperative Housing Development Association, 1973); and J. Robert Dodge, *Cooperative Housing*, Ideas and Methods Exchange no. 52 (Washington, D.C.: U.S. Department of Housing and Urban Development, 1971).

in isolation. In addition to using public land for low-income housing, the Housing and Development Board has coordinated an extensive program of land reclamation, urban renewal, and slum clearance. The urban environment of Singapore has been transformed within a decade. Private construction for middle- and high-income groups has been encouraged by a mix of policies relating to zoning, taxation, and the construction materials industry. There has been some cross-subsidy through the provision of flats of different sizes and prices, but long-term subsidies for the program as a whole are not foreseen.

The increase of 155,000 units in the overall housing stock in a population consisting of some 450,000 households has resulted in a trickle-down effect to the poor through reduced rents for housing of lower quality. This effect, however, has been in part offset by the massive slum clearance that accompanied high-rise construction, and the housing task that Singapore set for itself remains incomplete.

Hong Kong's experience is generally similar to that of Singapore in that it represents an effective use of a mix of general as well as housing-related public policies to provide efficient housing for the bulk of the population. The Hong Kong Housing Authority constructed nearly 35,000 units housing 220,000 persons between 1954 and 1972. As in Singapore, large-scale public housing efforts are a part of a total development strategy.

There are also some significant differences, however. Hong Kong's housing projects were begun during a period of relatively low per capita income and most were carried out during a period in which the city's population doubled, from 2 million to more than 4 million.[7] Thus, housing was for the most part designed to reach families with lower incomes than in Singapore. Hong Kong had a much greater problem in matching potential housing solutions with its resources. The earliest programs were developed to resettle squatters made homeless by fire. These were followed by general resettlement projects and early efforts to meet the needs of low-income families not living in squatter areas. Only then were programs introduced to assist families that had incomes above the maximum qualifying level for low-income housing but not high enough to compete effectively in the private housing market.

Space and service standards adopted for Hong Kong's early projects were well below limits previously considered acceptable in the city. In the beginning, large families occupied single, small rooms, and more

---

7. In 1960, per capita GNP in Hong Kong was only US$410, compared with US$720 in 1970. Singapore's per capita GNP was US$480 in 1960, US$920 in 1970.

than sixty families shared water supply and sanitary facilities. Standards were thus not geared to what was desirable but to what was affordable by the public purse and by families with severely limited incomes. Recognizing the substandard nature of the accommodation provided and expecting future economic improvement, the authorities took pains to design the buildings for ready conversion. By tearing out walls, each living unit could be expanded. After twenty years some of the blocks have been converted to provide more than double the original space per family unit, as well as private sanitary facilities.

The policy in both Singapore and Hong Kong has held that housing cost should represent a low proportion of household income. With rising incomes over the years, rents have been increased in real terms. Although these increases have been moderate and have lagged behind the increase in the opportunity cost of the public capital invested in housing, the fact that rents have been increased at all tends to reaffirm the general policy of gearing housing standards to ability to pay. Housing programs have changed with the improved economic status of Singapore and Hong Kong. The gradual raising of standards is an aspect of housing planning that reflects the benefits of industrialization and rising per capita income.

Both Singapore's and Hong Kong's housing programs have been integrated with efforts to provide accessible employment. In Singapore "flatted factories"[8] for small-scale industry have been built in the middle of housing developments, and large-scale, labor-intensive industries have been attracted by the provision of factory space for leasing in the midst of housing estates. In Hong Kong early public housing schemes were also developed with the construction of flatted factories. This was partly an outcome of the resettlement policy, which required relocation of squatter workshops. Later, new industrial sites were located near housing developments. Housing projects at first faced a shortage of schools, shops, day-care centers, and clinics. Progressively stronger support for community facilities was built into the programs, and today complete communities rather than isolated housing estates are developed. In cases in which the new communities are located in outlying areas, public transport is provided from the outset. The implementation of these policies is economically feasible because of the large number of people housed at one location. There are small settle-

---

8. These factories, five to seven stories high in Hong Kong, provide factory space in standard units for the manufacture of a variety of goods. Built within housing estates, factory blocks provide employment for residents of the estate and for those persons awaiting new housing after demolition and clearance of their squatter huts.

ments of 20,000 people, but more recently clusters of 55,000 have been considered as minimal, and these have been placed in newly constructed districts of up to 1 million people. Private and social costs, particularly those relating to transport, have been significantly reduced. In addition, the unusually good public transport systems support a wide range of choice in employment.

The shortage of land suitable for housing and commercial uses common to both cities was especially acute in Hong Kong, which is characterized by steep slopes that contribute to the high cost of grading and site development. Land reclamation, which serves the needs of both housing and industry, has consequently been an essential part of Hong Kong's urban and economic planning, and it has also played an important role in Singapore. The high-density use of the land created for housing, as well as commercial and industrial uses, has made the high cost of reclamation economic.

In both Hong Kong and Singapore the financial arrangements for housing have respected tenants' incomes while being provident of public funds. These arrangements provide for the write-down, or reduction, in value of public land and low interest rates on loan capital. A revolving housing fund has been established in Hong Kong for programs directed toward families with incomes above the maximum for lowest-income housing.[9] Families with insufficient income to pay rent—even with the land and interest subsidies—are eligible for rent subsidies.

The scale and nature of the housing effort has enabled it to take a part in stimulating the overall growth of the two cities. Ample provision has been made for retail traders, including attempts in Singapore to give hawkers greater security and opportunity for increased income. Carrying out the housing program gave experience to local contractors, who were then able to undertake other major construction projects. Singapore has also used housing construction to dampen the cyclical fluctuations of its open economy.

The construction and maintenance of this volume of housing requires considerable technical expertise in the public sector. With a significant increase in acquired skills and with the changes in programs, the Hong Kong and Singapore governments have built housing institutions with wide-ranging expertise. The programs in each city were

9. The financing of Hong Kong's housing policies is made possible through the use of two sources of income in addition to the traditional revenues available to other governments: income from the sale of leases of public land to private developers for commercial, industrial, and residential development; and income from port operations and other public enterprises, including the licensing of the private companies that run public transport.

initially organized by a number of separate authorities, but they are now administered by a single housing agency that is responsible for all public housing and community developments from the planning stage through execution to management.

Without adequate managerial expertise, the high housing densities of these programs probably would have created great difficulties. The housing management profession is relatively unknown, even in countries with extensive public housing. Much of the problem of tenant delinquency, for example, has been attributed to a lack of adequate systems for rent collection.[10] Singapore has opted for private ownership, in part to help overcome management problems. Hong Kong has fashioned its own housing management needs after the British model and now trains the required personnel at the University of Hong Kong.

Conclusions

Because public authorities are involved in housing from many different perspectives, it matters a great deal where this involvement takes place and how it is conceived and carried out. Where the capacity to save is limited, sites-and-services or squatter-upgrading programs allow urban families to acquire a piece of land and to build on it according to their own timetable and financial capacity. Well-designed projects of this type also allow for a variety of income levels, opening possibilities of financing through cross-subsidization. Cooperative housing, though not often directly benefiting the poor, promotes a sense of community self-reliance—as, for example, when neighbors pool their skills to complete an access road or drainage canal.

As illustrated by the experience of Singapore and Hong Kong, well-conceived and -managed public housing programs also have a role to play. Of course, the precise form of Singapore's and Hong Kong's public housing would not be suitable for all cities and all countries. Just as Hong Kong and Singapore found individual solutions to their particular housing problems, so do or so can other cities and countries.

The experience of these two cities indicates, however, that the principal ingredients of success in public housing are known. Housing standards must be consistent with prevailing income levels, but buildings have to be designed flexibly, at first to low standards, so that they can be adapted as incomes rise. Design and construction must be technically sound and economically efficient. Public housing must be well

10. W. Grindley and R. Merrill, *Sites and Services: The Experience and Potential* (Washington, D.C.: World Bank, May 1973; processed).

located in relation to job opportunities. Principal family income earners should have reasonable access to major areas of employment. Employment has to be available, preferably nearby, for secondary family workers. A housing area must be large enough to have community facilities such as schools, health clinics, markets, shops, and recreation areas—or to have good access to them. It appears to be somewhat easier to manage owned than rental units, but in either case the management input must be substantial and efficient. Such management not only must deal with matters of finance and maintenance, but also may need to employ social workers to assist families to deal with adjustment to high-density housing and other problems, and staff to collect rental or time payments according to a predetermined schedule. To be effective, public housing must have most of these components in a form that meets the needs and cultural patterns of the occupants.

Statistical Appendix

Table A1. Population Growth, Income, and Housing Indicators for Selected Cities

Part A. Population growth

Country[a]	City	City population, 1970 Thousands of persons[a]	City population, 1970 As percent of urban population of country	Annual percentage growth of city, 1960–70	Urban population as percent of total population of country, 1970
Relatively high-income countries					
Venezuela	Caracas	2,290	32	5.3	76
	Maracaibo	727	10	5.3	76
	Barquisimeto	293	4	4.0	76
	Ciudad Guayana	133	2	3.8[b]	76
Panama	Panama City	418	62	4.9	47
Chile	Santiago	2,623	38	3.1	74
Hong Kong	Hong Kong	3,550	97	2.9	100
Mexico	Mexico City	3,026	11	2.3	58
Lebanon	Beirut	700	61	2.9	40
Singapore	Singapore	2,072	100	2.6	100
Middle-income countries					
Zambia	Lusaka	279	27	6.4[b]	26
Ivory Coast	Abidjan	437	44	7.6	29
Korea	Seoul	5,536	46	6.7	39
	Busan	1,881	16	3.2	39
Malaysia	Kuala Lumpur[c]	741	46	5.5	46
Honduras	Tegucigalpa	232	35	5.9	36
Philippines	Manila[c]	2,942	22	4.3	23
Peru	Lima	2,877	42	5.1	46
	Arequipa	195	28	3.9	46
	Chimbote	103	15	3.3[b]	46
Brazil	Rio de Janeiro	4,252	8	4.4	54
	Belo Horizonte	1,106	2	8.3	54
	Recife	1,046	2	4.9	54
	Porto Alegre	870	2	7.5	54
	Brasilia	272	1	13.5	54
Colombia	Bogotá	2,463	19	7.3	55
	Cali	874	6	6.5	55
	Buenaventura	119	1	5.0[b]	55
Iraq	Bagdad[c]	2,055	49	4.4	44
Ecuador	Guayaquil	742	31	5.9	38
Senegal	Dakar	650	66	6.0	27
Guatemala	Guatemala City	778	49	5.0	37

Note: In most cases population data are for the cities rather than metropolitan areas. The city populations are used where data for slums and squatter settlements are available for cities only.

a. Figures refer to population within municipal boundaries (unless otherwise indicated) and thus represent varying proportions of total urban populations. Their usefulness for comparative purposes is therefore in this sense restricted.

b. Growth rate of urban population of country.

c. Metropolitan areas.

Table A1 (continued)

Part A (continued)

Country[a]	City	City population, 1970		Annual percentage growth of city, 1960–70	Urban population as percent of total population of country, 1970
		Thousands of persons[a]	As percent of urban population of country		
Middle-income countries (continued)					
Turkey	Ankara	1,209	9	5.9	31
	Istanbul	2,247	17	6.8	31
	Izmir	521	4	7.6	31
Ghana	Accra	865	30	6.8	34
Jordan	Amman	478	45	4.5	44
Liberia	Monrovia	96	63	10.4[b]	30
Morocco	Casablanca	1,445	31	4.2	35
	Rabat	485	10	9.2	35
Cameroon	Douala[c]	250	20	4.1	13
	Yaoundé	165	13	6.8[b]	13
Poorest countries					
Sri Lanka	Colombo	590	24	2.8	17
India	Calcutta[c]	6,881	6	1.8	19
	Bombay	5,839	5	2.2	19
	Delhi[c]	3,524	3	3.0	19
	Madras	2,416	2	2.2	19
	Baroda	450	0.5	3.6	19
Pakistan	Karachi	3,442	25	5.6	16
Afghanistan	Kabul[c]	483	36	3.2	7
Indonesia	Jakarta	4,174	21	4.7	18
	Bandung	1,098	5	4.6	18
	Makassar	555	3	3.9	18
Kenya	Nairobi	535	48	6.2	9
	Mombasa	255	23	5.8	9
Togo	Lomé	148	58	8.2	17
Malagasy	Tananarive[c]	358	32	5.6	11
Nigeria	Ibadan	736	6	3.0	21
Sudan	Port Sudan	106	7	3.5	8
Tanzania	Dar es Salaam	334	43	9.0	8
Zaïre	Kinshasa	1,331	21	3.4	17
Ethiopia	Addis Ababa	737	35	3.9	7
Malawi	Blantyre	160	54	10.1[b]	5
Nepal	Katmandu	240	36	7.9[b]	5
Somalia	Mogadishu	206	35	6.0[b]	24
Upper Volta	Ouagadougou	101	50	7.1[b]	5

(Table continues on the following page.)

113

Table A1 (continued)

Part B. Income and Income Distribution

Country	City	GNP per capita, 1970 (U.S. dollars)	Percentage of national income received by lowest 40 percent of households in country[e]	Gini coefficient[d]		
				Of entire country	Of urban population	Of rural population
Relatively high-income countries						
Venezuela	Caracas	980	15.7	0.5240 H	0.4194 H	0.4419 H
	Maracaibo	980	15.7	0.5240 H	0.4194 H	0.4419 H
	Barquisimeto	980	15.7	0.5240 H	0.4194 H	0.4419 H
	Ciudad Guayana	980	15.7	0.5240 H	0.4194 H	0.4419 H
Panama	Panama City	730	15.7	0.5368 E	0.3459 H	n.a.
Chile	Santiago	720	15.7	0.4868 H	0.4335 H	0.4103 H
Hong Kong	Hong Kong	970	15.7	0.4300	0.4300 H	n.a.
Mexico	Mexico City	670	9.5	0.5580 H	0.4487 H	0.5125 H
Lebanon	Beirut	590	9.5	0.5175 H	n.a.	n.a.
Singapore	Singapore	920	9.5	n.a.	n.a.	n.a.
Middle-income countries						
Zambia	Lusaka	400	16.3	0.4881 H	n.a.	n.a.
Ivory Coast	Abidjan	310	16.3	0.4325 P	n.a.	n.a.
Korea	Seoul	250	16.3	0.3923 P	n.a.	n.a.
	Busan	250	16.3	0.3923 P	n.a.	n.a.
Malaysia	Kuala Lumpur[c]	380	12.8	0.3633 H	0.4593 H	0.4988 H
Honduras	Tegucigalpa	280	12.8	0.5979 H	0.4833 H	0.4645 H
Philippines	Manila[c]	210	12.8	0.4955 H	n.a.	n.a.
Peru	Lima	450	8.5	0.5714 E	n.a.	n.a.
	Arequipa	450	8.5	0.5714 E	n.a.	n.a.
	Chimbote	450	8.5	0.5714 E	n.a.	n.a.
Brazil	Rio de Janeiro	420	8.5	0.5534 H	0.5327 H	0.4729 H
	Belo Horizonte	420	8.5	0.5534 H	0.5327 H	0.4729 H
	Recife	420	8.5	0.5534 H	0.5327 H	0.4729 H
	Porto Alegre	420	8.5	0.5534 H	0.5327 H	0.4729 H
	Brasilia	420	8.5	0.5534 H	0.5327 H	0.4729 H
Colombia	Bogotá	340	8.5	0.5417 E	0.5231 H	0.4527 H
	Cali	340	8.5	0.5417 E	0.5231 H	0.4527 H
	Buenaventura	340	8.5	0.5417 E	0.5231 H	0.4527 H
Iraq	Bagdad[c]	320	8.5	0.6068 P	n.a.	n.a.

n.a. Not available.

c. Metropolitan areas.

d. The Gini coefficient is the ratio of the area lying between the Lorenz curve and the 45-degree line of equal incomes to the area formed by the Lorenz curve and the x- and y-axes. Inequality increases as the coefficient approaches unity, decreases as it approaches zero. H indicates survey of "households"; P, of "population"; and E, of "economically active population." (The definitions of each category are not necessarily identical for every survey.)

e. Rough averages for groups of countries.

Country	City	GNP per capita, 1970 (U.S. dollars)	Percentage of national income received by lowest 40 percent of households in country[e]	Gini coefficient[d]		
				Of entire country	Of urban population	Of rural population
Middle-income countries (continued)						
Ecuador	Guayaquil	290	8.5	0.6567 E	0.5071 H	0.6008 E
Senegal	Dakar	230	8.5	0.5640 P	n.a.	n.a.
Guatemala	Guatemala City	360	n.a.	n.a.	n.a.	n.a.
Turkey	Ankara	310	n.a.	n.a.	n.a.	n.a.
	Istanbul	310	n.a.	n.a.	n.a.	n.a.
	Izmir	310	n.a.	n.a.	n.a.	n.a.
Ghana	Accra	310	n.a.	n.a.	n.a.	n.a.
Jordan	Amman	250	n.a.	n.a.	n.a.	n.a.
Liberia	Monrovia	240	n.a.	n.a.	n.a.	n.a.
Morocco	Casablanca	230	n.a.	n.a.	n.a.	n.a.
	Rabat	230	n.a.	n.a.	n.a.	n.a.
Cameroon	Douala[c]	180	n.a.	n.a.	n.a.	n.a.
	Yaoundé	180	n.a.	n.a.	n.a.	n.a.
Poorest countries						
Sri Lanka	Colombo	110	15.2	0.3730 H	0.4080 H	0.3405 H
India	Calcutta[c]	110	15.2	0.3988 H	0.4532 H	0.3523 H
	Bombay	110	15.2	0.3998 H	0.4532 H	0.3523 H
	Delhi[c]	110	15.2	0.3998 H	0.4532 H	0.3523 H
	Madras	110	15.2	0.3998 H	0.4532 H	0.3523 H
	Baroda	110	15.2	0.3998 H	0.4532 H	0.3523 H
Pakistan	Karachi	100	15.2	0.3588 H	0.4825 H	0.3395 H
Afghanistan	Kabul[c]	80	15.2	n.a.	n.a.	n.a.
Indonesia	Jakarta	80	15.2	n.a.	n.a.	n.a.
	Bandung	80	15.2	n.a.	n.a.	n.a.
	Makassar	80	15.2	n.a.	n.a.	n.a.
Kenya	Nairobi	150	16.0	n.a.	n.a.	n.a.
	Mombasa	150	16.0	n.a.	n.a.	n.a.
Togo	Lomé	140	16.0	n.a.	n.a.	n.a.
Malagasy	Tananarive[c]	130	16.0	n.a.	n.a.	n.a.
Nigeria	Ibadan	120	16.0	n.a.	n.a.	n.a.
Sudan	Port Sudan	120	16.0	0.4279 H	n.a.	n.a.
Tanzania	Dar es Salaam	100	16.0	0.5040 P	n.a.	n.a.
Zaïre	Kinshasa	90	16.0	n.a.	n.a.	n.a.
Ethiopia	Addis Ababa	80	16.0	n.a.	n.a.	n.a.
Malawi	Blantyre	80	16.0	n.a.	n.a.	n.a.
Nepal	Katmandu	80	16.0	n.a.	n.a.	n.a.
Somalia	Mogadishu	70	16.0	n.a.	n.a.	n.a.
Upper Volta	Ouagadougou	60	16.0	n.a.	n.a.	n.a.

(Table continues on the following page.)

Table A1 (continued)
Part C. Housing

Country	City	Residential construction As percent of country GDP	Residential construction As percent of country GDCF[f]	Gross population density of city (persons per square kilometer)	Urban housing condition in country[g]	Slums and squatter settlements as percent of city population[h]	
Relatively high-income countries							
Venezuela	Caracas	4.32	17.74	1,186	n.a.	40	(1969)
	Maracaibo	4.32	17.74	n.a.	n.a.	50	(1969)
	Barquisimeto	4.32	17.74	n.a.	n.a.	41	(1969)
	Ciudad Guayana	4.32	17.74	n.a.	n.a.	40	(1969)
Panama	Panama City	4.40	20.96	197	38.3 (1960)	17	(1970)
Chile	Santiago	2.82	18.79	n.a.	14.7 (1970)	25	(1964)
Hong Kong	Hong Kong	n.a.	n.a.	n.a.	n.a.	16	(1969)
Mexico	Mexico City	n.a.	n.a.	n.a.	47.4 (1960)	46	(1970)
Lebanon	Beirut	n.a.	n.a.	n.a.	n.a.	1.5	(1970)
Singapore	Singapore	n.a.	n.a.	n.a.	n.a.	15	(1970)
Middle-income countries							
Zambia	Lusaka	n.a.	n.a.	n.a.	n.a.	48	(1969)
Ivory Coast	Abidjan	n.a.	n.a.	n.a.	n.a.	60	(1964)
Korea	Seoul	2.71	10.93	9,031	58.9 (1960)	30	(1970)
	Busan	2.71	10.93	n.a.	58.9 (1960)	31	(1970)
Malaysia	Kuala Lumpur[c]	n.a.	n.a.	n.a.	n.a.	37	(1971)
Honduras	Tegucigalpa	n.a.	n.a.	n.a.	n.a.	25	(1970)
Philippines	Manila[c]	n.a.	n.a.	5,116	30.1 (1967)	35	(1972)
Peru	Lima	n.a.	n.a.	4,380	33.7 (1961)	40	(1970)
	Arequipa	n.a.	n.a.	n.a.	33.7 (1961)	40	(1970)
	Chimbote	n.a.	n.a.	n.a.	n.a.	67	(1970)
Brazil	Rio de Janeiro	n.a.	n.a.	n.a.	2.8 (1969)	30	(1970)
	Belo Horizonte	n.a.	n.a.	n.a.	2.8 (1969)	14	(1970)
	Recife	n.a.	n.a.	n.a.	2.8 (1969)	50	(1970)
	Porto Alegre	n.a.	n.a.	n.a.	2.8 (1969)	13	(1970)
	Brasilia	n.a.	n.a.	n.a.	2.8 (1969)	41	(1970)
Colombia	Bogotá	3.76	20.01	n.a.	n.a.	60	(1969)
	Cali	3.76	20.01	n.a.	n.a.	30	(1969)
	Buenaventura	3.76	20.01	n.a.	n.a.	80	(1969)
Iraq	Bagdad[c]	n.a.	n.a.	n.a.	n.a.	29	(1965)
Ecuador	Guayaquil	n.a.	n.a.	n.a.	39.9 (1962)	49	(1969)
Senegal	Dakar	n.a.	n.a.	n.a.	n.a.	60	(1971)
Guatemala	Guatemala City	n.a.	n.a.	n.a.	n.a.	30	(1971)

n.a. Not available.

c. Metropolitan areas.

f. Gross domestic capital formation.

g. Percentage of occupied dwellings with three or more persons a room in urban areas.

h. These figures are notional since definitions vary widely across countries; they are used to indicate rough orders of magnitude.

Part C (continued)

Country	City	Residential construction As percent of country GDP	As percent of country GDCF[f]	Gross population density of city (persons per square kilometer)	Urban housing condition in country[g]	Slums and squatter settlements as percent of city population[h]
Middle-income countries (continued)						
Turkey	Ankara	3.97	22.16	n.a.	29.2 (1965)	60 (1970)
	Istanbul	3.97	22.16	n.a.	29.2	40 (1970)
	Ismir	3.97	22.16	n.a.	29.2	65 (1970)
Ghana	Accra	4.76	40.95	n.a.	n.a.	53 (1968)
Jordan	Amman	n.a.	n.a.	n.a.	n.a.	14 (1971)
Liberia	Monrovia	n.a.	n.a.	n.a.	n.a.	50 (1970)
Morocco	Casablanca	n.a.	n.a.	n.a.	34.4 (1971)	70 (1971)
	Rabat	n.a.	n.a.	n.a.	34.4 (1971)	60 (1971)
Cameroon	Douala[c]	n.a.	n.a.	n.a.	n.a.	80 (1970)
	Yaoundé	n.a.	n.a.	n.a.	n.a.	90 (1970)
Poorest countries						
Sri Lanka	Colombo	n.a.	n.a.	n.a.	n.a.	43 (1968)
India	Calcutta[c]	n.a.	n.a.	n.a.	n.a.	33 (1971)
	Bombay	n.a.	n.a.	n.a.	n.a.	25 (1971)
	Delhi[c]	n.a.	n.a.	n.a.	n.a.	30 (1971)
	Madras	n.a.	n.a.	n.a.	n.a.	25 (1971)
	Baroda	n.a.	n.a.	n.a.	n.a.	19 (1971)
Pakistan	Karachi	n.a.	n.a.	n.a.	59.0 (1960)	23 (1970)
Afghanistan	Kabul[c]	n.a.	n.a.	n.a.	n.a.	21 (1971)
Indonesia	Jakarta	n.a.	n.a.	n.a.	n.a.	26 (1972)
	Bandung	n.a.	n.a.	n.a.	n.a.	27 (1972)
	Makassar	n.a.	n.a.	n.a.	n.a.	33 (1972)
Kenya	Nairobi	2.92	15.88	n.a.	41.1 (1962)	33 (1970)
	Mombasa	2.92	15.88	n.a.	41.1 (1962)	66 (1970)
Togo	Lomé	n.a.	n.a.	n.a.	n.a.	75 (1970)
Malagasy	Tananarive[c]	n.a.	n.a.	n.a.	n.a.	33 (1969)
Nigeria	Ibadan	n.a.	n.a.	n.a.	n.a.	75 (1971)
Sudan	Port Sudan	n.a.	n.a.	n.a.	n.a.	55 (1971)
Tanzania	Dar es Salaam	n.a.	n.a.	n.a.	n.a.	50 (1970)
Zaïre	Kinshasa	n.a.	n.a.	6,589	n.a.	60 (1969)
Ethiopia	Addis Ababa	n.a.	n.a.	n.a.	n.a.	90 (1968)
Malawi	Blantyre	n.a.	n.a.	n.a.	n.a.	56 (1966)
Nepal	Katmandu	n.a.	n.a.	n.a.	20.2	22 (1961)
Somalia	Mogadishu	n.a.	n.a.	n.a.	n.a.	77 (1967)
Upper Volta	Ouagadougou	n.a.	n.a.	n.a.	n.a.	70 (1966)

Sources: S. Jain and A. E. Tiemann, "Size Distribution of Income: Compilation of Data," Staff Working Paper no. 190 (Washington, D.C.: World Bank, 1973); L. Grebler, "The Role of Housing in Economic Development," (paper prepared for the Third World Conference of Engineers and Architects, Tel Aviv, December 1973); *World Bank Atlas* (Washington, D.C., 1973); and United Nations, *World Housing Survey* (New York, January 1974).

Table A2. Housing Indicators for Selected Developing Countries
Part A. Relatively High-Income Countries

Country[a]	Per capita GNP, 1970 (U.S. dollars) (1)	Slums and uncontrolled settlements		Migration		Dwellings completed per 1,000 persons 1960-70		Average annual urban growth rate 1960-70 (percent) (8)	Annual growth rate of principal city, 1960-70 (percent) (9)
		City (2)	Percentage of total population (3)	Year (4)	As percentage of urban growth (5)	Minimum (6)	Maximum (7)		
Relatively high income									
Venezuela	980	Caracas	40	1960-66	50	3.3	4.2	5.6	5.5
Cyprus	950							3.9	
Romania	930								
Singapore	920		15			6.0	8.5	2.6	2.6
Trinidad and Tobago	860					2.0	4.5	6.0	
Uruguay	820							2.9	4.7
Panama	730	Panama City	17					4.4	4.9
Chile	720	Santiago	25			2.2	5.4	3.4	3.1
Mexico	670	Mexico City	46					5.2	5.0
Jamaica	670	Kingston	25					4.3	5.0
Portugal	660							1.7	1.2
Yugoslavia	650							4.8	3.7
Gabon	630							6.5	
Lebanon	590	Beirut	15					4.0	
Costa Rica	560							4.6	3.4
Bahrain	550								5.4

Table A2 (continued)

Part A (continued)

Country[a]	Principal city as percentage of urban population, 1970 (10)	National labor force in construction		Construction value added as a percentage of GDP, 1970 (13)	Gini coefficient[b]	
		Year (11)	Percentage (12)		Year (14)	Coefficient (15)
Venezuela	22	1971	6.5	5.1	1962	0.5240 H
Cyprus		1960	8.7			
Romania		1966	5.2			
Singapore	100	1957	5.1			
Trinidad and Tobago		1960	10.8			
Uruguay	63	1963	5.5	2.9	1967	0.4153 H
Panama	64				1969	0.5368 E
Chile	37	1971	8.3	4.0	1968	0.4868 H
Mexico	12	1970	4.4	5.1	1969	0.5580 H
Jamaica	77	1960	7.6		1958	0.5581 H
Portugal		1960	6.7			
Yugoslavia	15	1961	3.8	12.5	1968	0.3333 H
Gabon		1963	1.7		1960	0.6505 P
Lebanon	58				1955–60	0.5175 H
Costa Rica	68	1963	5.9		1971	0.4286 H
Bahrain		1971	17.3			

a. By income group and in descending order of 1970 gross national product per capita.
b. For a definition of "Gini coefficient" and of the abbreviations used, see Table A1, note d.

(Table continues on the following page.)

Table A2 (continued)

Part B. Middle-Income Countries

Country[a]	Per capita GNP, 1970 (U.S. dollars) (1)	Slums and uncontrolled settlements		Migration		Dwellings completed per 1,000 persons 1960–70		Average annual urban growth rate 1960–70 (percent) (8)	Annual growth rate of principal city, 1960–70 (percent) (9)
		City (2)	Percentage of total population (3)	Year (4)	As percentage of urban growth (5)	Minimum (6)	Maximum (7)		
Peru	450	Lima	40					3.3	5.1
Saudi Arabia	440								
Nicaragua	430							4.6	5.9
Fiji	430							3.9	
Brazil	420	Rio de Janeiro	30					4.6	6.4
Zambia	400	Lusaka	48	1964	85			6.4	
China (Taiwan)	390							4.1	4.7
Malaysia	380	Kuala Lumpur	37	1947–57	50			5.9	4.0
Iran	380							4.8	6.0
Guyana	370					2.7	5.6	3.2	3.1
Guatemala	360	Guatemala City	30					4.9	5.0
Dominican Republic	350					0.4	0.9	5.7	5.9
Oman	350								
Colombia	340	Bogotá	60			1.0	1.4	5.0	7.0
Iraq	320	Bagdad	29			1.7	2.2	4.0	4.4

Country		City		Period					
Turkey	310	Istanbul	40	1960–65	50			4.2	5.0
Ivory Coast	310	Abidjan	60	1955–63	76			9.3	11.0
Ghana	310	Accra	53					6.8	6.8
Congo	300							5.4	4.0
El Salvador	300							4.0	4.6
Algeria	300					0.7	1.0	4.7	5.9
Ecuador	290	Guayaquil	49					3.4	2.4
Syria	290							5.2	5.9
Honduras	280	Tegucigalpa	25					3.5	3.6
Paraguay	260								
Jordan	250	Amman	14					4.8	4.5
Korea, Republic of	250	Seoul	30	1955–65	63			4.1	8.0
Tunisia	250					1.0	1.8	3.2	0.8
Liberia	240	Monrovia	50					10.4	
Mauritius	240					2.7	12.1	5.3	
Morocco	230	Casablanca	70					4.9	4.2
Senegal	230	Dakar	60					4.0	6.0
Egypt	210					0.9	1.8	4.0	4.1
Equatorial Guinea	210					0.1	0.6		
Philippines	210	Manila	35					4.3	4.3
South Vietnam	200								
Thailand	200							4.5	6.0
Sierra Leone	190							3.8	
Bolivia	180							2.4	2.3
Cameroon	180	Douala	80					6.8	4.0
Swaziland	180							9.4	

a. By income group and in descending order of 1970 gross national product per capita.

121

(Table continues on the following page.)

Table A2 (continued)

Part B (continued)

Country[a]	Principal city as percentage of urban population, 1970 (10)	National labor force in construction		Construction value added as a percentage of GDP, 1970 (13)	Gini coefficient[b]	
		Year (11)	Percentage (12)		Year (14)	Coefficient (15)
Peru	40			5.0	1970–71	0.5714 E
Saudi Arabia	40					
Nicaragua		1971	3.7			
Fiji		1966	5.8			
Brazil	17			1.2	1970	0.5534 H
Zambia	20			7.9	1959	0.4881 H
China (Taiwan)	23					
Malaysia	15	1966	6.7	4.0	1957–58	0.3633 H
Iran	29	1965	5.2			
Guyana	41					
Guatemala	41	1964	2.6	1.8		
Dominican Republic	41	1960	2.5	5.4		
Oman						
Colombia	22	1964	4.3	5.3	1970	0.5417 E
Iraq	32	1957	4.5		1956	0.6068 P

Country		Year			Year	Gini coefficient
Turkey	24	1965	2.6	7.9	1959	0.4325 P
Ivory Coast	25	1964	0.9	6.1		
Ghana		1960	3.3			
Congo	27					
El Salvador		1961	4.1		1969	0.4508 P
Algeria	36	1966	5.0	4.5		
Ecuador	28	1962	3.2		1970	0.6567 E
Syria		1969	3.2		1967–68	0.5979 H
Honduras	40	1961	2.0			
Paraguay	52	1962	3.3			
Jordan	33	1961	10.3			
Korea, Republic of	37			6.4	1970	0.3923 P
Tunisia	33	1966	6.4	8.5	1961	0.4975 P
Liberia		1962	2.9	4.8		
Mauritius	31	1962	10.6			
Morocco	27	1960	1.7	5.2	1960	0.5640 P
Senegal	52			3.5		
Egypt	38			4.8		
Equatorial Guinea						
Philippines	46	1970	3.8	2.6	1965	0.4955 H
South Vietnam						
Thailand	45	1960	0.5	6.1	1962	0.4964 H
Sierra Leone	49	1963	1.7	4.1		
Bolivia	50	1950	2.4	4.6		
Cameroon				7.2		
Swaziland	31					

123

a. By income group and in descending order of 1970 gross national product per capita.
b. For a definition of "Gini coefficient" and of the abbreviations used, see Table A1, note d.

(Table continues on the following page.)

Table A2 (continued)

Part C. Lowest-Income Countries

| Country[a] | Per capita GNP, 1970 (U.S. dollars) (1) | Slums and uncontrolled settlements | | Migration | | Dwellings completed per 1,000 persons 1960–70 | | Average annual urban growth rate 1960–70 (percent) (8) | Annual growth rate of principal city, 1960–70 (percent) (9) |
		City (2)	Percentage of total population (3)	Year (4)	As percentage of urban growth (5)	Minimum (6)	Maximum (7)		
Kenya	150	Nairobi	33	1963–73	50			5.1	6.0
Togo	140	Lomé	75					8.2	
Central African Republic	140							8.4	
Mauritania	140							2.4	
Malagasy Republic	130	Tananarive	33					4.3	5.6
Khmer Republic	130					0.2	0.2	4.8	7.6
Uganda	130							9.2	9.2
Laos	120								
Sudan	120							4.3	3.4
Guinea	120							6.6	7.0
Yemen (People's Democratic Republic)	120							4.2	
Gambia	120							3.8	
Nigeria	120			1952–62	75			6.0	
India	110	Calcutta	33					2.9	1.8
Sri Lanka	110	Colombo	43			0.8	1.5	3.6	2.8
Botswana	110							3.3	
Haiti	110								

124

Pakistan	100	Karachi	23	4.3		5.6
Tanzania	100	Dar es Salaam	50	8.6		9.0
Zaïre	90	Kinshasa	60	3.9		10.0
Lesotho	90			7.9		
Benin	90			6.0		
Niger	90			2.4		
Afghanistan	80	Kabul	21	2.3		3.2
Chad	80			7.0		
Ethiopia	80	Addis Ababa	90	2.4	1.0	3.9
Burma	80					
Malawi	80	Blantyre	56	10.1		
Nepal	80	Katmandu	22	8.0		7.9
Indonesia	80	Jakarta	26	4.2		4.7
Yemen (Arab Republic)	80			5.9		
Mali	70			5.7		5.6
Somalia	70	Mogadishu	77	6.0		
Burundi	60			7.2		
Rwanda	60			8.3		
Upper Volta	60	Ouaga- dougou	70	5.1		

125

a. By income and in descending order of 1970 gross national product per capita.

(Table continues on the following page.)

Table A2 (continued)

Part C (continued)

Country[a]	Principal city as percentage of urban population, 1970 (10)	National labor force in construction		Construction value added as a percentage of GDP, 1970 (13)	Gini coefficient[b]	
		Year (11)	Percentage (12)		Year (14)	Coefficient (15)
Kenya	50			5.8		
Togo	59					
Central African Republic	15					
Mauritania						
Malagasy Republic	48					
Khmer Republic	80					
Uganda	53			1.9	1970	0.3817[c]
Laos						
Sudan	34	1956	0.6		1963	0.4279 H
Guinea	49					
Yemen (People's Democratic Republic)		1958 (?)	13.8			
Gambia						
Nigeria	6	1961	1.1	4.5		
India	5	1963	2.5	2.8	1964–65	0.3998 H
Sri Lanka	60			6.6	1969–70	0.3730 H
Botswana		1964	1.1			
Haiti		1950	0.6		1963–64	0.3713 H

Pakistan	18	2.1	1968	4.9	1963–64	0.3588 H
Tanzania	33			4.7	1967	0.5040 P
Zaïre	19			6.0	1959	0.4370 P
Lesotho						
Benin						
Niger	44				1960	0.3570 P
Afghanistan						
Chad					1958	0.3545 P
Ethiopia	38			5.6	1958	
Burma						0.3720 H
Malawi	73					
Nepal	80	0.1	1961			
Indonesia	21	1.3	1964–65	2.8	1958	
Yemen (Arab Republic)		13.8	1958 (?)			
Mali	28			5.7		
Somalia						
Burundi						
Rwanda						
Upper Volta						

a. By income group and in descending order of 1970 gross national product per capita.
b. For a definition of "Gini coefficient" and of the abbreviations used, see Table A1, note d.
c. African adult male employees.

Sources: *World Bank Atlas 1972* (Washington, D.C.: World Bank, 1972); United Nations, *World Housing Survey* (New York: U.N., January 1974); *Urbanization Sector Working Paper* (World Bank, June 1972); Robert S. McNamara, "Promotion of Domestic Construction Industries in Developing Countries" memo from the president (World Bank, July 12, 1973); and S. Jain and A. E. Tiemann, "Size Distribution of Income; Compilation of Data," World Bank Staff Working Paper no. 190 (Washington, D.C.: World Bank, 1973).

127

Table A3. Public Expenditure on Housing, Selected Developing Countries, Various Years

| | | Housing as percentage of | |
| | | Total public expenditure[a] | GNP |
Country	Year		
Algeria[b]	1970	0.7	0.2
Barbados[c]	1971–72	4.4[d]	1.3
Brazil	1971	6.9	0.9
Colombia[c]	1972	3.5[e]	n.a.
Dominican Republic	1971	4.5	0.9
Guyana	1971	0.1	n.a.
Honduras	1970	2.4[f]	0.4
Hong Kong	1971	6.1	0.9
Ireland[g]	1970–71	5.4[h]	2.0
Israel	1970–71	0.1[i]	n.a.
Jamaica	1971–72	2.3	0.6
Kenya[j]	1971–72	2.0[k]	0.6
Korea	1970	0.2	n.a.
Malawi	1969	1.5	n.a.
Malaysia	1971	0.9	0.2
Mauritius	1970–71	0.5[l]	0.1
Morocco[c]	1970	0.4	0.1
Panama	1970	1.5[m]	0.4
Paraguay	1972	0.4[n]	n.a.
Peru	1971	0.5	0.1
Sri Lanka	1969–70	1.1	0.3
Trinidad and Tobago	1970	2.8[o]	0.6
Venezuela	1970	6.6[p]	1.5

n.a. Not available.

a. Figures represent central government expenditures except as otherwise noted.

b. Public sector expenditures, consisting of central government, state-owned banking institutions, state enterprises, and self-managed agricultural units.

c. Includes town planning, urban development, or both.

d. Central government makes grants to a decentralized housing authority, which provides loans for low-cost housing, and to the Urban Development Corporation, which supervises urban development schemes and middle-income housing services.

e. Housing and community development are the responsibility mainly of decentralized agencies, which have their own revenues but also receive national government grants.

f. Provided mainly by the National Housing Institute, a decentralized agency that receives grants from the central government and can borrow from the private sector and from abroad.

g. Mainly expenditures of local authorities. Details are as follows (in millions of pounds): local housing authority, 16.7; housing grants and loans, 16.1; National Building Agency Ltd., 0.5; and independent development company scheme, 1.1; for a total housing expenditure of 34.4.

h. Figure represents expenditures of central budget agencies as well as local authorities and state bodies covered in capital budget.

i. Central government provides housing loans to immigrants and the poor, which are not included.

j. Includes statutory boards and parastatal bodies of a regulatory nature.

k. Includes loans and grants to the National Housing Corporation.

l. Housing services are provided by the Central Housing Authority and the Mauritius Housing Corporation, both public corporations; figures include central government grants to these two agencies.

m. Transfers to Housing Institute and Mortgage Institute, both public corporations.

n. Provided by a public corporation, which receives central government grants.

o. The National Housing Authority, a public corporation, is responsible for low-cost housing and slum clearance; it is partly financed with central government grants.

p. Provided mainly through grants to public corporations and autonomous local government agencies.

Sources: Kazuko K. Artus with Orani Dixon and Rosamund Weatherall, "Cross-Country Data on Government Expenditure Classified by Functions," Studies in Domestic Finance no. 3, Development Economics Department (Washington, D.C.: World Bank, December 1973; processed); and Roy W. Bahl and Elliott R. Morss, "The Urban Lending Program of the World Bank: The Case for Comparative Urban Information" (Washington, D.C.: World Bank, February 1974; processed).

Table A4. Housing in the Economy: Significant Regression Results of Preliminary Tests[a]

Preferred form	Dependent variable[b]	Constant	Independent variable[b]	Regression coefficient	$\bar{R}^2$	S.E.E.	Degrees of freedom
Linear	SLUMPOP	0.495 (15.4)	CITYPOP	−0.00005 (−3.0)	0.11	0.19	64
Linear	SLUMPOP	0.494 (12.5)	GNPCAPT	−0.0002 (−2.1)	0.05	0.20	64
Linear	SLUMPOP	0.52 (11.6)	URBPOP	−0.265 (−2.5)	0.07	0.20	64
Linear	CPOPURB	0.07 (2.3)	PRINCITY	0.329 (8.09)	0.49	0.16	64
Linear	URBPOP	0.09 (4.9)	GNPCAPT	0.0007 (17.6)	0.82	0.10	64
Linear	URBPOP	−0.20 (−1.1)	GINI	1.235 (3.3)	0.21	0.18	36
Log	URBPOP	−2.59 (−5.0)	CITYPOP	0.197 (2.5)	0.08	0.73	64
Linear	CPOPURB	1.11 (2.8)	GINIURB	−1.99 (−2.4)	0.16	0.21	24
Log	URBPOP	1.25 (2.5)	GINIRUR	2.55 (4.5)	0.45	0.41	22
Log	SLUMPOP	−2.77 (−3.3)	DENSITY	0.226 (2.2)	0.35	0.33	6
Log	CPOPURB	−4.49 (−9.6)	HOUSING	0.823 (5.6)	0.59	0.77	20
Linear	URBPOP	0.509 (7.6)	HOUSING	−0.0044 (−2.3)	0.17	0.16	20
Log	HOUSING	6.53 (5.8)	RCGDCF	−1.046 (−2.6)	0.43	0.32	7

a. Equations significant at 0.05 level or higher. Figures in parentheses are t-statistics.
b. Variables tested:

Urbanization
URBPOP: population of urban areas as percentage of total population.

Urban primacy
CPOPURB: population of city as percentage of population of urban areas.

Severity of housing problem
SLUMPOP: percentage of city population living in slums.
HOUSING: percentage of dwellings with three or more persons per room in all urban areas of country.

Population
CITYPOP: population of city.
POPGR; average annual growth rate of city.
DENSITY: gross population density of city.
PRINCITY: principal city, dummy variable.

Income level and distribution
GNPCAPT: country per capita GNP.
GDPCITY: city per capita GDP.
GINI: Gini ratio, country.
GINIURB: Gini ratio, all urban areas of country.
GINIRUR: Gini ratio, all rural areas of country.

Relative importance of housing
RCGDP: residential construction as percentage of country GDP.
RCGDCF: residential construction as percentage of country gross domestic fixed capital formation.

Table A5. Number and Population of Urban Areas by Size Class for Income Groups of Developing Countries, 1970

| Income group | Population size of urban areas | | | | | | | | Total number of urban areas | Total population (thousands) |
| | 0.2–0.5 million | | 0.5–1.0 million | | 1.0–2.0 million | | 2.0 million and over | | | |
	Number of urban areas	Total population (thousands)	Number of urban areas	Total population (thousands)	Number of urban areas	Total population (thousands)	Number of urban areas	Total population (thousands)		
Relatively high[a]	12	6,215	5	3,224	6	7,746	5	14,506	28	31,691
Middle[b]	73	20,992	28	19,146	9	13,040	12	47,140	122	100,318
Lowest[c]	76	23,370	28	18,303	9	13,007	6	25,896	119	80,576
Total	161	50,577	61	40,673	24	33,793	23	87,542	269	212,585

a. GNP per capita, 1970, US$450–1,000; thirteen countries.
b. GNP per capita, 1970, US$150–450; thirty-four countries.
c. GNP per capita, 1970, US$150 and under; thirty-one countries.
Source: Kingsley Davis, World Urbanization 1950–1970, vol. I: Basic Data for Cities (Berkeley, Calif.: University of California Press, 1969).

Table A6. Cost of Residential Construction, Utilities, and Land Development, and of Land for Low- and Medium-Density Housing, Selected Developing Countries

| | | Cost per square meter, 1970 prices (U.S. dollars) | | |
Country[a]	GNP per capita, 1970 (U.S. dollars)	Basic construction	Utilities and land development	Land[b]
Kuwait	3,860	64.86	5.19	1.68
Venezuela	980	34.00	7.00	n.a.
Trinidad and Tobago	860	33.00	7.40	n.a.
Uruguay	820	33.00	2.00	n.a.
Chile	720	42.00	3.90	n.a.
Mexico	670	40.00	4.10	n.a.
Jamaica[c]	670	73.60	4.74	6.63
Lebanon	590	32.52	2.82	4.00
Costa Rica	560	30.00	3.70	n.a.
Peru	450	47.00	6.30	n.a.
Saudi Arabia	440	48.41	3.87	2.77
Brazil	420	35.00	4.30	n.a.
Guatemala	360	25.00	3.50	n.a.
Colombia	340	24.00	5.90	n.a.
Iraq	320	35.84	2.87	0.70
El Salvador	300	29.00	4.90	n.a.
Ecuador	290	33.00	3.10	n.a.
Syria	290	32.25	2.58	2.41
Jordan	250	39.69	3.18	1.40
Korea	250	61.00[d]	3.97[e]	2.25
Philippines	210	51.03	1.50	5.18
Bolivia	180	26.00	1.70	n.a.
Sri Lanka	110	42.33	3.36	1.00
India	110	25.00	1.65	0.49
Bangladesh	100	n.a.	4.20	0.84
Pakistan	100	n.a.	2.50	0.62

n.a. Not available.
a. In descending order of gross national product per capita.
b. Located at periphery of the city.
c. Kingston.
d. Seoul.
e. Gwangju.

Sources: Latin America, Foundation for Cooperative Housing, *Cooperative Housing and the Minimum Shelter Approach in Latin America*; Middle East and Asia, "Study of International Housing, Reports from U.S. Agencies and International Organizations," prepared for the Subcommittee on Housing and Urban Affairs of the Committee on Banking, calculated from Housing and Urban Affairs, U.S. Senate (Washington, D. C., June 28, 1971), pp. 228–29. Jamaica and Korea data supplied by respective governments.

Table A7. Cost of Basic Construction, Land Servicing, and Raw Land as a Percentage of Total Housing Cost for Low- and Moderate-Income Housing,[a] Selected Cities

City	Housing type[b]	Costs for low-income housing			Costs for moderate-income housing		
		Basic construction[c]	Land servicing[d]	Raw land[e]	Basic construction[c]	Land servicing[d]	Raw land
Ahmedabad	S	n.a.	n.a.	n.a.	68.7 (5)	8.4	22.9[f]
	M	84.1 (1)	8.6	7.3	77.5 (4)	8.0	14.5[f]
Bogotá	S	69.5 (11)	12.2	18.3	78.5 (15)	9.1	12.4[e]
	M	91.5 (14)	3.8	4.7	95.6 (16)	1.9	2.5[e]
Hong Kong[g]	M	68.1 (27)		29.4	n.a.	n.a.	n.a.
Madras	S	48.1 (30)	23.0	28.9	n.a.	n.a.	n.a.
	M	76.9 (31)	12.4	10.7	80.4	6.1	13.5[f]
Mexico City	S	44.9 (34)	9.3	45.8	58.8	3.8	37.4[e]
	M	79.9 (36)	6.3	13.8	80.1	4.7	15.2[e]
Nairobi	S	64.5 (42)	21.5	14.0	n.a.	n.a.	n.a.
Seoul[g]	M	n.a.	n.a.	n.a.	71.4 (52)	15.0	6.9[e]

n.a. Not available.
a. With individual toilet and services.
b. S = Single family; M = multifamily.
c. Figure in parenthesis indicates type of unit described in appropriately numbered row in Table A13.
d. Includes utilities and land development.
e. Located at periphery of the city.
f. Located inside the city.
g. Percentages do not add up to 100 because administrative cost is not included.
Source: Table A13. Data for moderate-income housing from C. Araud and others, Studies on Employment in the Mexican Housing Industry (Paris: Organization for Economic Cooperation and Development, 1973), pp. 70–90.

Table A8. Land Price Variations, Selected Cities, Various Years
(Current U.S. dollars per square meter)

City[a]	Year	Population (millions)	Price of land[b]		
			Periphery	Intermediate zone	Central business district, commercial
Seoul	1973	6.2	2.3	75.0	1,060.0[c]
Manila	1973	5.1	2.0	60.0–75.0	450.0–1,500.0[c]
Hong Kong	1973	4.2	84.5–126.8	127.4–255.0	1,275.0
Madras	1973	2.6	4.4–5.5	6.6	8.5–13.6
Bogotá	1970	2.5	3.6	32.0	130.0
Singapore	1973	2.3	45.0	140.0	3,275.0[c]
Ahmedabad	1973	1.7	3.0–4.0	24.0–29.0	22.0–44.0
Kinshasa	1971	1.5	0.5	9.0	150.0[c]
Abidjan	1972	0.6	0.4	9.0	139.0[c]
Gwangju	1973	0.6	0.75	28.0	114.0[c]
Nairobi	1972	0.6	6.9	3.1–14.9	210.9–361.6

a. In descending order of population.
b. Actual or calculated market value.
c. Maximum.
Sources: Korea, Korea Board of Appraisers and World Bank mission data; Philippines, Manila, Board of Real Estates Association; Hong Kong, New Territories Administration; Madras, Tamil Nadu Housing Board; Bogotá, estimate from sample information; Singapore, Trade and Industry, various issues; Ahmedabad, Gujarat Housing Board; Zaïre, Bureau d'Etudes d'Amenagements Urbains; Ivory Coast, Ministry of Finance; Nairobi, University of Nairobi, Department of Land Development.

Table A9. Cost of Basic Construction, Land Servicing, and Raw
Land for Low- and Moderate-Income Housing, Selected Cities
(U.S. dollars, 1970 prices)

City	Cost of		
	Basic construction of housing unit per square meter of livable space	Land servicing per square meter of livable space[a]	Raw land per square meter
Ahmedabad	25.5–61.1	2.6–7.5	2.3–19.5
Bogotá	20.5–109.3	1.1–6.1	3.6–4.2
Hong Kong		41.5–133.5[b]	60.3–75.7
Madras	15.7–59.4	4.1–9.3	3.4–5.1
Mexico City	28.5–49.6	3.9–5.9	7.4–14.1
Nairobi	48.9–65.3	12.0–21.7	1.9–4.3
Seoul	55.7–69.2	5.4–5.8	6.7–8.1

a. Includes utilities and land development.
b. Includes share of cost for community facilities such as schools and community centers.
Source: Table A13.

*Table A10. Indexes of Costs of Various Housing Components,
Bogotá, Yearly, 1969–73
(1967–68 = 100)*

Component	1969	1970	1971	1972	1973
Basic materials					
Steel	121.20	143.04	156.01	169.43	196.74
Cement	111.68	133.66	144.79	161.27	178.90
Electricity installation	110.83	120.87	133.86	152.18	200.63
Sanitary installation	107.86	122.38	135.31	146.38	170.60
Brick	102.00	105.11	117.13	182.08	261.55
Timber	122.10	146.78	159.97	165.77	190.29
Stone	114.22	118.58	124.47	141.92	154.55
Paint	115.16	115.16	127.07	139.64	162.80
Weighted average, basic materials	114.77	132.16	145.84	162.95	185.96
Labor					
Total	111.16	126.66	160.82	187.55	205.63
Weighted average, all components	113.83	130.50	148.22	170.37	192.10

Source: Cámara Colombiana de la Construcción, *Boletín Mensual de Estadística no. 40.* Bogotá, March 1974.

134

*Table A11. Indexes of Costs of Various Housing Components,
Nairobi, 1966 and Yearly, 1970–73*
(1968 = 100)

Component	1966	1970	1971	1972	1973
Basic materials					
Ballast	53.6	94.0	104.0	95.0	95.0
Stone[a]	63.0	74.0	85.0	85.1	139.0
Sand	63.9	111.0	116.0	127.3	139.0
Cement	98.8	100.0	100.0	100.0	120.0
Mild steel rod[b]	n.a.	101.5	134.0	95.3	254.0
Timber	74.6	107.1	114.0	114.1	114.0
Labor					
Skilled	69.4	111.1	111.0	111.2	152.0
Semiskilled	93.1	128.0	111.0	111.3	128.0
Unskilled	83.0	110.4	111.0	111.0	128.0

n.a. Not available.
a. 230 by 230 millimeters.
b. 12 millimeters.
Source: Republic of Kenya, *Economic Survey 1974* (Nairobi: Central Bureau of Statistics, Ministry of Finance and Planning, June 1974), p. 111.

Table A12. Trends in Costs of Housing Components,
Selected Countries, 1960, 1965, and 1970
(U.S. dollars per square meter)[a]

Country	Component	Costs per square meter of built-up area		
		1960	*1965*	*1970*
Bangladesh	Materials	15.36	n.a.	n.a.
	Labor	7.78	n.a.	n.a.
	Subtotal	23.15	26.94	31.51
	Management	5.80	n.a.	n.a.
	Total	28.95	n.a.	n.a.
India	Materials	20.00	24.21	18.66
	Labor	7.36	9.47	6.66
	Subtotal	27.36	33.68	25.32
	Management	5.80	n.a.	n.a.
	Total	33.16	n.a.	n.a.
Iraq	Materials	21.89	19.65	20.80
	Labor	9.64	10.71	11.78
	Subtotal	31.53	30.36	32.59
	Management	3.15	3.04	33.25
	Total	34.68	33.40	35.84
Jordan	Materials	21.70	21.33	22.16
	Labor	11.42	12.49	13.92
	Subtotal	33.12	33.82	36.08
	Management	3.31	3.38	3.61
	Total	36.43	37.20	39.69
Kuwait	Materials	34.63	35.00	36.11
	Labor	18.92	20.71	22.85
	Subtotal	53.55	55.71	58.96
	Management	5.35	5.57	5.90
	Total	58.90	61.28	64.86
Lebanon	Materials	14.47	13.54	13.90
	Labor	14.99	16.42	18.21
	Subtotal	29.46	29.96	32.11
	Management	2.94	2.99	3.21
	Total	32.40	32.95	35.32

n.a. Not available.
a. Exchange rate for each year. Prices for 1970 were estimated at the exchange rate for 1969.

Table A12 (continued)

Country	Component	Costs per square meter of built-up area		
		1960	*1965*	*1970*
Pakistan	Materials	11.15	n.a.	n.a.
	Labor	5.60	n.a.	n.a.
	Subtotal	16.80	22.60	28.30
	Management	4.20	n.a.	n.a.
	Total	21.00	n.a.	n.a.
Philippines	Materials	22.40	19.84	32.42
	Labor	9.60	8.50	13.98
	Subtotal	32.00	28.34	46.40
	Management	3.20	2.83	4.63
	Total	35.20	31.17	41.03
Saudi Arabia	Materials	18.65	20.62	23.30
	Labor	17.14	18.92	20.71
	Subtotal	35.79	39.54	44.01
	Management	3.58	3.95	4.40
	Total	39.37	43.49	48.41
Sri Lanka	Materials	21.05	25.15	23.52
	Labor	10.52	12.57	11.76
	Subtotal	31.57	37.72	35.28
	Management	6.31	7.54	7.05
	Total	37.88	45.26	42.33
Syria	Materials	18.12	18.41	18.25
	Labor	9.28	9.99	11.07
	Subtotal	27.40	28.40	29.32
	Management	2.74	2.84	2.93
	Total	30.14	31.24	32.25

Source: "Study of International Housing, Reports from U. S. Agencies and International Organizations," prepared for the Subcommittee on Housing and Urban Affairs of the Committee on Banking, Housing and Urban Affairs, United States Senate (Washington, D. C., June 26, 1971), pp. 228–29.

Table A13. Comparison of Quality and Estimated Cost of Selected Housing Units for Low- and Moderate-Income Housing, Selected Cities

Type of housing and year	Number of stories	Area per unit (square meters) Shelter	Area per unit (square meters) Land[a]	Gross density, dwelling units per hectare	Sewerage and water	Electricity	Roads
Ahmedabad							
1. Integrated subsidized housing scheme, 1973	4	20	20	n.a.	✔	✔	✔
2. Low-income group housing scheme, 1973	4	33	50	n.a.	✔	✔	✔
3. Middle-income group housing scheme, 1973	4	65	60	n.a.	✔	✔	✔
4. Private multifamily housing, 1974	2–4	65	30	n.a.	✔	✔	✔
5. Private single-family housing, 1974	1	65	80	n.a.	✔	✔	✔
Bogotá							
6. Sites and services, 1970, public	1	n.a.	75	75			
7. Sites and services, 1970, public	1	n.a.	75	75	✔		
8. Sites and services, 1970, public	1	n.a.	75	75	✔	✔	
9. Sites and services, 1970, public	1	n.a.	75	75	✔	✔	✔
10. Sites and services, 1970, public	1	n.a.	75	75	✔	✔	✔
11. Single-family social, 1970, public	1	50	75	75	✔	✔	✔
12. Single-family modest, 1970, public	1	50	91	54	✔	✔	✔
13. Single-family modest, 1970, public	1–2	50	91	54	✔	✔	✔
14. Multifamily model, 1970, public	1–5	50	30	160	✔	✔	✔
15. Single-family medium, 1970, public	1–2	100	180	31	✔	✔	✔
16. Multifamily medium, 1970, public	1–5	100	60	91	✔	✔	✔
17. Multifamily medium, 1970, public	1–5	100	38	144	✔	✔	✔
18. Inquilinato	1	12	n.a.	n.a.	✔[f]	✔[f]	
19. CVP (Caja de la Vivienda Popular), Type A, Site only, 1974	1		64	n.a.	✔[f]	✔[f]	✔
20. CVP, Type B, 1974 Core housing	1	12	64	n.a.		✔	
21. CVP, Type C, 1974	1	25	64	n.a.	✔	✔	✔
22. CVP, Type D, 1974	1	40	64	n.a.	✔	✔	✔
23. Private developer A, single family	1	130	200	n.a.	✔	✔	✔
24. Private developer B, single family	1	130	423	n.a.	✔	✔	✔

n.a. Not available.
a. For multifamily units, share of land per housing unit.
b. Includes utilities and land development.

Table A13 (continued)

	Cost components (current U.S. dollars)						
Livable space per square meter			Per unit costs				
Land servicing[b]	Basic construction[c]	Raw land per square meter	Land servicing[b]	Basic construction[c]	Raw land	Total
Ahmedabad						
1. 3.5	34.6	3.0	71	692	60	823
2. 6.7	43.5	4.1	221	1,438	206	1,865
3. 6.7	40.9	3.0	435	2,658	236	3,329
4. 6.7	65.6	26.0[d]	435	4,264	780	5,479
5. 10.0	81.3	22.0[d]	650	5,284	1,760	7,694
Bogotá						
6. 0.4[e]	0	3.6	30	0	270	300
7. 1.0[e]	0	3.6	75	0	270	345
8. 1.7[e]	0	3.6	128	0	270	398
9. 2.0[e]	0	3.6	150	0	270	420
10. 2.4[e]	0	3.6	180	0	270	450
11. 3.7	20.5	3.6	180	1,025	270	1,475
12. 6.1	31.6	4.2	305	1,580	382	2,267
13. 6.1	33.3	4.2	305	1,665	382	2,352
14. 2.0	49.1	4.2	101	2.455	126	2,682
15. 5.0	43.3	3.8	504	4,330	684	5,518
16. 1.7	86.5	3.8	168	8,650	228	9,046
17. 11.1	109.3	3.8	107	10,930	144	11,181
18. n.a.	n.a.	n.a.	n.a.	n.a.	n.a.	803[g]
19. 4.9[h]	0	4.6	314[i]	0	294	635[g]
20. 4.9[e]	29.4	4.6	314	353	294	980[g]
21. 14.1[i]	33.7	4.6	353[i]	843	294	1,569[g]
22. 10.8[i]	27.0	4.6	431[i]	1,078	294	1,922[g]
23. n.a.	n.a.	n.a.	n.a.	n.a.	n.a.	21,687
24. n.a.	n.a.	n.a.	n.a.	n.a.	n.a.	23,695

c. Construction of housing unit and internal services.
d. Assumes intermediate location.
e. Cost per square meter of plot.

(Table continues and other notes are shown on the following page.)

139

Table A13 (continued)

Type of housing and year	Number of stories	Area per unit (square meters) Shelter	Area per unit (square meters) Land[a]	Gross density, dwelling units per hectare	Services Sewerage and water	Services Electricity	Services Roads
Hong Kong							
25. Low-cost housing estate (Ngau Tau Kok), 1970[j]	10+	18–34	n.a.	1,160	✔	✔	✔
26. Housing authority estate (Pink Shek), 1971[j]	10+	25–31	n.a.	790	✔	✔	✔
27. Housing authority estate (Wah Fu), 1972[j]	10+	25–34	n.a.	660	✔	✔	✔
28. Housing authority estate (Oi Man), 1974[j]	10+	23–40	n.a.	710	✔	✔	✔
Madras							
29. Open-plot scheme, 1966	n.a.		90	n.a.	n.a.	n.a.	n.a.
30. Public housing A, 1973	1	17.5	50[k]	n.a.	✔	✔	✔
31. Public housing B, 1973	4	23.2	25[k]	n.a.	✔	✔	✔
32. Private housing C, 1973	2	19.1	40[k]	n.a.	✔	✔	✔
33. Private housing D, 1973	5+	20.0	40[k]	n.a.	✔	n.a.	n.a.
Mexico City							
34. Minimum-cost single family (average unit), 1970	1–2	47.3	186	n.a.	✔	✔	✔
35. Low-cost single family (average unit), 1970	1–2	71.6	183	n.a.	✔	✔	✔
36. Low-cost multifamily (average unit), 1970	4–5	67.3	41	n.a.	✔	✔	✔
Nairobi							
37. Site scheme, fence only, 1974	n.a.	n.a.	125[m]	65	✔[n]		✔
38. Sites and services A, pit latrine, 1974	n.a.	1.4	125[m]	65	✔[n]		✔
39. Sites and services B, toilet and shower, 1974	1	4.2	125[m]	65	✔		✔
40. Core housing A, toilet, shower, stove, kitchen, 1974	1	11.7	150[m]	55	✔		✔

n.a. Not available.
a. For multifamily units, share of land per housing unit.
b. Includes utilities and land development.
c. Construction of housing unit and internal services.
d. Assumes intermediate location.
e. Cost per square meter of plot.
f. Communal services only.
g. Includes administrative costs.

	Cost components (current U.S. dollars)						
Livable space per square meter			Per unit costs				
Land servicing[b]	Basic construction[c]	Raw land per square meter	Land servicing[b]	Basic construction[c]	Raw land	Total
Hong Kong							
25.	41.5	60.3		1,037	532	1,670[g]
26.	51.2	81.7		1,280	1,027	2,380[g]
27.	71.7	46.5		1,793	776	2,633[g]
28.	167.5	95.7		4,188	1,340	6,421[g]
Madras							
29. 2.3[e]	0	0.6	210	0	54	264
30. 10.0	20.9	4.4[l]	175	366	220	761
31. 5.5	34.1	4.4[l]	128	791	110	1,029
32. 10.0	52.8	6.6[d]	191	1,008	264	1,463
33. 6.0	78.6	6.6[d]	120	1,572	264	1,956
Mexico City							
34. 5.9	28.5	7.4	280	1,349	1,376	3,005
35. 4.9	49.3	13.1	351	3,530	2,398	6,279
36. 3.9	49.6	14.1	263	3,338	578	4,179
Nairobi							
37. 0.9[e]	0.5[e]	3.1	112	56	388	556
38. 0.9[e]	1.8[e]	3.1	112	224	388	724
39. 4.8[e]	5.5[e]	3.1	605	684	388	1,677
40. 60.8	113.9	3.1	712	1,333	465	2,510

h. Cost per square meter of plot; cost for roads not included.
i. Cost for roads not included.
j. Cost estimates are based on total project costs, which include housing, services, and commercial and community facilities.
k. Assumes average size plot.
l. Assumes location at periphery.

(Table continues on the following page.)

Type of housing and year	Number of stories	Area per unit (square meters) Shelter	Area per unit (square meters) Land[a]	Gross density, dwelling units per hectare	Sewerage and water	Elec- tricity	Roads
						Services	

Nairobi (continued)

Type of housing and year	Number of stories	Shelter	Land[a]	Gross density	Sewerage and water	Elec-tricity	Roads
41. Core housing B, toilet, shower, stove, kitchen, roof, and concrete strip for one room, 1974	1	19.2	150[m]	55	✔		✔
42. Core housing C, one-room house, 1974	1	20.5	150[m]	55	✔		✔
43. Two-room house A, 1974	1	32.9	150[m]	55	✔	✔	✔
44. Two-room house B, 1974	1	33.7	150[m]	55	✔	✔	✔
45. Three-room house, 1974	1	42.5	150[m]	55	✔	✔	✔
46. Self-help housing A, Kiberia Experimental Scheme, 1974	1	17.9	150[m]	55	✔	✔	✔
47. Self-help housing B, Kiberia Experimental Scheme, 1974	1	35.3	150[m]	55	✔	✔	✔
48. Self-help housing C, Kiberia Experimental Scheme, 1974	1	41.7	150[m]	55	✔	✔	✔
49. Self-help housing D, Kiberia Experimental Scheme, 1974	1	47.7	150[m]	55	✔	✔	✔
Seoul							
50. Korea Housing Corporation, condominium A, 1972[p]	5–6	76	93	107	✔	✔	✔
51. Korea Housing Corporation, condominium B, 1974[p]	5–6	43	37	268	✔	✔	✔
52. Korea Housing Corporation, condominium C, 1974[p]	5–6	50	43	233	✔	✔	✔

n.a. Not available.
a. For multifamily units, share of land per housing unit.
b. Includes utilities and land development.
c. Construction of housing unit and internal services.
e. Cost per square meter of plot.
g. Includes administrative costs.

Table A13 (continued)

			Cost components (current U.S. dollars)				
Livable space per square meter			Per unit costs				
Land servicing[b]	Basic construction[c]	Raw land per square meter	Land servicing[b]	Basic construction[c]	Raw land	Total	
Nairobi (continued)							
41. 37.1	82.6	3.1	712	1,585	465	2,762	
42. 34.7	104.6	3.1	712	2,145	465	3,322	
43. 24.9	79.9	6.9	818	2,628	1,035	4,481	
44. 24.3	98.7	6.9	818	3,327	1,035	5,180	
45. 19.2	83.5	6.9	818	3,550	1,035	5,403	
46. 39.8[o]	42.3	3.1[o]	712	758	465	1,935	
47. 23.0[o]	30.5	6.9[o]	818	1,050	1,035	2,903	
48. 19.5[o]	28.1	6.9[o]	818	1,176	1,035	3,029	
49. 17.0[o]	26.5	6.9[o]	818	1,260	1,035	3,113	
Seoul							
50. 11.6	70.0	15.1	880	5,320	1,488	9,000[g]	
51. 8.6	102.9	10.6	319	4,413	395	5,500[g]	
52. 29.8	122.6	13.6	1,277	6,068	585	8,500[g]	

m. Size of plot based on average size of housing unit built in 1968–70.

n. Water supply only.

o. Actual raw land and land servicing costs for Kiberia Experimental Scheme are not available. Estimates here assume land servicing and raw land costs are equivalent for housing types in rows 42 and 43, above.

p. Financed by USAID housing guaranty loan.

Table A14. Size Distribution and Average of Monthly Household Income, Selected Cities

Monthly household income class (current U.S. dollars)	Ahmedabad, 1970[a]		Bogotá, 1970		Hong Kong, 1971		Madras, 1970[b]		Mexico City, 1969		Nairobi, 1970		Seoul, 1970[c]	
	Per cent	Cumulative per cent	Per cent	Cumulative per cent	Per cent	Cumulative per cent	Per cent	Cumulative per cent	Per cent	Cumulative per cent	Per cent	Cumulative per cent	Per cent	Cumulative per cent
0–20.0			3.0	3.0	2.5	2.5			1.0	1.0	8.6	8.6	2.4	2.4
20.1–50.0			17.2	20.2	5.7	8.2			1.8	2.8	25.4	34.0	3.6	6.0
50.1–100.0			31.1	52.3	26.2	34.4			23.7	26.5	28.2	62.2	34.2	40.2
100.1–200.0			23.5	75.8	41.3	75.7			31.6	58.1	17.6	79.8	48.0	88.2
200.1–300.0			8.7	84.5	13.3	89.0			13.1	71.2	11.5	91.3	11.8[d]	100.0
300.1–400.0			2.8	87.3	4.6	93.6			10.8	82.0	2.3	93.6		
400.1 and over			12.7	100.0	6.4	100.0			28.8	100.0	6.4	100.0		
0–10.0	10.5	10.5					1.5	1.5						
10.1–20.0	22.1	32.6					20.9	22.4						
20.1–30.0	21.4	54.0					27.3	49.7						
30.1–50.0	22.5	76.5					30.8	80.5						
50.1–75.0	6.2	82.7					19.5[e]	100.0						
75.1–100.0	5.6	88.3												
100.1–150.0	8.3	96.6												
150.1–200.0	1.1	97.7												
200.1 and over	2.3	100.0												

144

Average monthly household income (U.S. dollars)	45	171	178	35	241	175	125

a. Estimate based on income distribution of urban population in Gujarat, assuming average income of households in Ahmedabad equal to 1.1 times that of households in all cities in Gujarat.

b. Estimate based on expenditure of urban households in Tamil Nadu, assuming average income of households in Madras equal to 1.1 times that of urban households in Tamil Nadu.

c. Estimate based on income distribution of wage and salary earner households in all cities in Korea, assuming average income of households in Seoul equal to 1.2 times that of households in all cities in Korea.

d. Over US$200.

e. Over US$50.

Sources: Mexico City, Secretaría de Industria y Comercio, Dirección General de Muestreo, *Ingresos y Egresos de las Familias en La República Mexicana 1969–1970,* vol. 1; Nairobi, "Home Interview Survey 1970," reported in K. J. Lewis, *Income Distribution in Nairobi* (Nairobi Urban Study Group, March 1973); Bogotá, projections prepared by Estudio de Desarrollo Urbano de Bogotá, Fase II; Hong Kong, *Hong Kong Population and Housing Census, 1971 Main Report* (government of Hong Kong Census and Statistics Department, 1972), chapter 8; Seoul, Korea, Economic Planning Board, *Annual Report on the Family Income and Expenditure Survey* (1970); Madras, V. Soundararajan, "A Note on Income Distribution and Levels of Living in Tamil Nadu" (State Planning Commission, 1971); Ahmedabad, National Council of Applied Economic Research, "Incidence of Taxation in Gujarat" (New Delhi) 1971, p. 80.

Table A15. Range of Monthly Household Income by Quintiles and Lowest Decile, Selected Cities

	Income range (current U.S. dollars a month)						
Household rank	Ahmedabad, 1970ᵃ	Bogotá, 1970	Hong Kong, 1971	Madras, 1970ᵇ	Mexico City, 1969	Nairobi, 1970	Seoul, 1970ᶜ
Lowest 10 percent	0–8.0	0–36.0	0–56.0	0–16.0	0–69.0	0–24.0	0–59.0
Lowest 20 percent	0–18.0	0–51.0	0–79.0	0–19.0	0–85.0	0–39.0	0–73.0
Second 20 percent	18.1–22.0	51.1–78.0	79.1–110.0	19.1–26.0	85.1–132.0	39.1–64.0	73.1–101.0
Third 20 percent	22.1–35.0	78.1–123.0	110.1–149.0	26.1–34.0	132.1–211.0	64.1–94.0	101.1–125.0
Fourth 20 percent	35.1–62.0	123.1–234.0	149.1–216.0	34.1–50.0	211.1–382.0	94.1–202.0	125.1–166.0
Highest 20 percent	62.1 and over	234.1 and over	216.1 and over	50.1 and over	382.1 and over	202.1 and over	166.1 and over

a. Estimate based on income distribution of urban population in Gujarat, assuming average income of households in Ahmedabad equal to 1.1 times that of households in all other cities in Gujarat.

b. Estimate based on expenditure of urban households in Tamil Nadu, assuming average income of households in Madras equal to 1.1 times that of urban households in Tamil Nadu.

c. Estimate based on income distribution of wage and salary earner households in all cities in Korea, assuming average income of households in Seoul equal to 1.2 times that of households in all other cities in Korea.

Source: Same as Table A14.

Table A16. *Percentage of Household Expenditure Devoted to*
Housing, Utilities, and Transport by Salary and Wage-earner
Households, Korean Cities, 1968–72

Item of expenditure	1968	1969	1970	1971	1972
Seoul					
Housing[a]	17.3	18.9	19.3	19.1	20.1
Utilities[b]	4.9	4.6	4.9	5.4	4.4
Transport[c]	4.6	5.4	5.9	5.7	5.9
Total	26.8	28.9	30.1	30.2	30.4
All cities					
Housing[a]	16.7	18.1	18.2	18.3	18.5
Utilities[b]	5.1	5.0	5.8	5.6	5.3
Transport[c]	3.8	4.3	4.7	4.2	4.5
Total	25.6	27.4	28.7	28.1	28.3

a. Includes imputed rent on owner-occupied dwellings.
b. Fuel and electricity.
c. Includes communication.
Source: Korea, Economic Planning Board, *Annual Report on the Family Income and Expenditure Survey* (Seoul: Economic Planning Board, 1969–73).

Table A17. Estimates of Construction Costs and Monthly Household Income Required to Purchase Housing of Various Standards and Locations, Mexico City (U.S. dollars, 1970 prices)

| Service standard[a] | Location[b] | Cost per housing unit | | | | Monthly payment[c] | Monthly household income required[d] | Percentage of households unable to afford |
		Raw land	Land servicing	Basic construction	Total			
Single-family dwelling[e]								
M	P	555	118	570	1,243	11.40	76	14
M	I	18,098	118	570	18,786	172.80	1,152	95+
M	C	255,750	118	570	256,438	2,359.20	15,728	95+
L	P	555	106	456	1,117	10.30	69	10
L	I	18,098	106	456	18,660	171.70	1,145	95+
L	C	255,750	106	456	256,312	2,358.10	15,721	95+
B	P	555	94	342	991	9.00	60	6
B	I	18,098	94	342	18,534	168.40	1,122	95+
B	C	255,750	94	342	256,186	2,327.90	15,520	95+

Multifamily dwelling[f]

M	P	111	78	992	1,181	10.71	71	12
M	I	3,615	78	992	4,685	42.60	284	72
M	C	51,150	78	992	52,220	474.50	3,163	95+
L	P	111	70	794	975	8.90	59	7
L	I	3,615	70	794	4,479	40.60	271	70
L	C	51,150	70	794	52,014	472.50	3,150	95+
B	P	111	62	595	768	7.00	47	4
B	I	3,615	62	595	4,272	38.70	258	69
B	C	51,150	62	595	51,807	470.70	3,138	95+

a. M (medium) = individual toilet and services. L (low) = four households sharing toilet and services. Assumes 10 percent saving in land servicing and 20 percent saving in basic construction costs. B (basic) = centrally located water and pit latrines. Assumes 20 percent saving in land servicing and 40 percent saving in basic construction costs.

b. P = peripheral area. I = intermediate zone. C = center of city.

c. Assumes a 25-year period of payment and 10 percent interest.

d. Assumes no down payment and 15 percent of household income devoted to housing.

e. 20 square meters of livable space and 75 square meters of land.

f. 20 Square meters of livable space and 15 square meters share of land.

Source: Costs of components per square meter, from Tables A9 to A13. Estimates of land prices from intermediate and central zones are based on rent gradient in Seoul.

149

Table A18. Estimates of Construction Costs and Monthly Household Income Required to Purchase Housing of Various Standards and Locations, Nairobi (U.S. dollars, 1970 prices)

Service standard[a]	Location[b]	Cost per housing unit				Monthly payment[c]	Monthly household income required[a]	Percentage of households unable to afford
		Raw land	Land servicing	Basic construction	Total			
Single-family dwelling[e]								
M	P	180	420	1,260	1,860	17.10	114	66
M	I	788	420	1,260	2,468	22.70	151	72
M	C	17,250	420	1,260	18,930	174.20	1,161	95+
L	P	180	378	1,008	1,566	14.40	96	59
L	I	788	378	1,008	2,174	20.00	133	69
L	C	17,250	378	1,008	18,636	171.60	1,144	95+
B	P	180	336	756	1,272	11.50	77	52
B	I	788	336	756	1,880	17.10	114	66
B	C	17,250	336	756	18,342	166.60	1,111	95+

Multifamily dwelling[f]

M	P	36	200	1,600	16.60	111	65
M	I	158	200	1,600	17.70	118	67
M	C	3,450	200	1,600	47.70	318	90
L	P	36	180	1,280	13.60	91	58
L	I	158	180	1,280	14.60	98	61
L	C	3,450	180	1,280	44.60	297	89
B	P	36	160	960	10.40	70	47
B	I	158	160	960	11.50	77	52
B	C	3,450	160	960	41.50	277	87

a. M (medium) = individual toilet and services. L (low) = four households sharing toilet and services. B (basic) = centrally located water and pit latrines. Assumes 20 percent saving in land servicing and 20 percent saving in basic construction costs. Assumes 10 percent saving in land servicing and 20 percent saving in basic construction costs. Assumes 20 percent saving in land servicing and 40 percent saving in basic construction costs.

b. P = peripheral area. I = intermediate zone. C = center of city.

c. Assumes a 25-year period of payment and 10 percent interest.

d. Assumes no down payment and 15 percent of household income devoted to housing.

e. 20 square meters of livable space and 75 square meters of land.

f. 20 square meters of livable space and 15 square meters share of land.

Sources: Tables A9 and A13.

151

Table A19. Estimates of Construction Costs and Monthly Household Income Required to Purchase Housing of Various Standards and Locations, Bogotá
(U.S. dollars, 1970 prices)

| Service standard[a] | Location[b] | Cost per housing unit | | | | Monthly payment[c] | Monthly household income required[a] | Percentage of households unable to afford |
		Raw land	Land servicing	Basic construction	Total			
Single-family dwelling[e]								
M	P	270	74	410	754	6.90	46	17
M	I	2,400	74	410	2,884	26.50	177	73
M	C	9,750	74	410	10,234	94.20	628	95+
L	P	270	67	328	665	6.10	41	14
L	I	2,400	67	328	2,795	25.70	171	72
L	C	9,750	67	328	10,145	93.10	622	95+
B	P	270	60	246	576	5.20	35	11
B	I	2,400	60	246	2,706	24.60	164	71
B	C	9,750	60	246	10,056	91.30	609	95+

152

Multifamily dwelling[f]

M	P	54	40	992	1,086	9.80	65	36
M	I	480	40	992	1,512	13.70	92	50
M	C	1,950	40	992	2,982	27.10	181	74
L	P	54	36	794	884	8.00	54	23
L	I	480	36	794	1,310	11.80	79	42
L	C	1,950	36	794	2,780	25.30	169	72
B	P	54	32	595	681	6.20	42	15
B	I	480	32	595	1,107	10.00	67	36
B	C	1,950	32	595	2,577	24.00	160	70

a. M (medium) = individual toilet and services. L (low) = four households sharing toilet and services. Assumes 10 percent saving in land servicing and 20 percent saving in basic construction costs. B (basic) = centrally located water and pit latrines. Assumes 20 percent saving in land servicing and 40 percent saving in basic construction costs.

b. P = peripheral area. I = intermediate zone. C = center of city.

c. Assumes a 25-year period of payment and 10 percent interest.

d. Assumes no down payment and 15 percent of household income devoted to housing.

e. 20 square meters of livable space and 75 square meters of land.

f. 20 square meters of livable space and 15 square meters share of land.

Source: Tables A9 and A13.

153

Table A20. Estimates of Construction Costs and Monthly Household Income Required to Purchase Housing of Various Standards and Locations, Ahmedabad (U.S. dollars, 1970 prices)

Service standard[a]	Location[b]	Cost per housing unit				Monthly payment[c]	Monthly household income required[d]	Percentage of households unable to afford
		Raw land	Land servicing	Basic construction	Total			
Single-family dwelling[e]								
M	P	173	100	258	531	4.90	33	58
M	I	1,530	100	258	1,888	17.40	116	91
M	C	1,905	100	258	2,263	20.80	139	95+
L	P	173	90	206	469	4.20	28	56
L	I	1,530	90	206	1,826	16.80	112	91
L	C	1,905	90	206	2,201	20.20	135	95+
B	P	173	80	155	408	3.70	25	51
B	I	1,530	80	155	1,765	16.00	107	91
B	C	1,905	80	155	2,140	19.40	129	95+

Multifamily dwelling[f]

M	P	35	52	518	605	5.50	36	64
M	I	306	52	518	876	7.90	53	76
M	C	381	52	518	951	8.60	57	79
L	P	35	42	414	491	4.50	30	58
L	I	306	42	414	762	6.90	46	72
L	C	381	42	414	837	7.60	50	75
B	P	35	31	311	377	3.40	23	41
B	I	306	31	311	648	3.80	26	55
B	C	381	31	311	723	6.50	43	70

a. M (medium) = individual toilet and services. L (low) = four households sharing toilet and services. Assumes 10 percent saving in land servicing and 20 percent saving in basic construction costs. B (basic) = centrally located water and pit latrines. Assumes 20 percent saving in land servicing and 40 percent saving in basic construction costs.

b. P = peripheral area. I = intermediate zone. C = center of city.

c. Assumes a 25-year period of payment and 10 percent interest.

d. Assumes no down payment and 15 percent of household income devoted to housing.

e. 20 square meters of livable space and 75 square meters of land.

f. 20 square meters of livable space and 15 square meters share of land.

Sources: Tables A9 and A13.

Table A21. Estimates of Construction Costs and Monthly Household Income Required to Purchase Housing of
Various Standards and Locations, Madras
(U.S. dollars, 1970 prices)

Service standard[a]	Location[b]	Cost per housing unit				Monthly payment[c]	Monthly household income required[a]	Percentage of households unable to afford
		Raw land	Land servicing	Basic construction	Total			
Single-family dwelling[e]								
M	P	285	150	312	747	6.90	46	77
M	I	375	150	312	837	7.70	51	81
M	C	638	150	312	1,100	10.10	67	88
L	P	285	135	250	670	6.20	41	73
L	I	375	135	250	760	7.00	47	78
L	C	638	135	250	1,023	9.40	63	87
B	P	285	120	187	592	5.40	36	68
B	I	375	120	187	682	6.20	41	73
B	C	638	120	187	945	8.50	57	82

Multifamily dwelling[f]

M	P	57	84	510	651	5.90	39	70
M	I	75	84	510	669	6.00	40	72
M	C	128	84	510	722	6.50	43	75
L	P	57	76	408	541	4.60	30	63
L	I	75	76	408	559	4.90	32	65
L	C	128	76	408	612	5.50	37	68
B	P	57	67	306	430	3.80	25	38
B	I	75	67	306	448	4.00	27	44
B	C	128	67	306	501	4.60	30	63

a. M (medium) = individual toilet and services. L (low) = four households sharing toilet and services. Assumes 10 percent saving in land servicing and 20 percent saving in basic construction costs. B (basic) = centrally located water and pit latrines. Assumes 20 percent saving in land servicing and 40 percent saving in basic construction costs.

b. P = peripheral area. I = intermediate zone. C = center of city.

c. Assumes a 25-year period of payment and 10 percent interest.

d. Assumes no down payment and 15 percent of household income devoted to housing.

e. 20 square meters of livable space and 75 square meters of land.

f. 20 square meters of livable space and 15 square meters of land.

Sources: Tables A9 and A13.

157

Table A22. Implied Subsidy in Provision of Housing to Low-Income Families, by Location, Selected Cities[a]

City	Single-family housing				Multifamily housing			
	Individual services, periphery	Individual services, intermediate	Basic services, periphery	Basic services, intermediate	Individual services, periphery	Individual services, intermediate	Basic services, periphery	Basic services, intermediate
Median income, lowest 40 percent of households								
Ahmedabad	44.9	84.5	27.0	83.1	50.9	65.8	20.6	28.9
Bogotá	-10.9	71.1	-47.1	68.9	21.9	44.1	-23.4	23.5
Madras	58.7	63.0	47.2	54.0	51.7	52.5	25.0	28.8
Mexico City	-11.8	92.6	-41.7	92.4	-19.0	70.1	-82.1	67.1
Nairobi	65.8	74.2	49.1	65.8	64.8	66.9	43.7	49.1
Median income, lowest 20 percent of households								
Ahmedabad	75.5	93.1	67.6	92.5	78.2	84.8	64.7	68.4
Bogotá	21.7	79.6	-3.8	78.1	44.9	60.6	12.9	46.0
Madras	65.2	69.8	55.6	61.3	59.3	60.0	36.8	40.0
Mexico City	9.2	94.0	-15.0	93.9	3.4	75.7	-47.8	73.3
Nairobi	79.0	84.1	68.7	78.9	78.3	79.7	65.4	68.7

a. The implied subsidy is defined as percent by which monthly income available for housing falls short of required monthly payment. Based on repayment period of 25 years, no down payment, and 15 percent of household income devoted to housing. Negative numbers denote percent by which income exceeds payment, implying no need for subsidy.
Sources: Tables A17 through A21.

Select Bibliography

Abrams, Charles. *Man's Struggle for Shelter in an Urbanizing World.* Cambridge, Mass.: M.I.T. Press, 1964.

Araud, C., and others. *Studies on Employment in the Mexican Housing Industry.* Paris: Organization for Economic Cooperation and Development, 1973.

Architects' Combine. *A Comparative Study of Low and High Rise Housing for the Low Income Group.* Bombay: The City and Industrial Development Corporation of Maharashtra, Ltd., March 1973.

Artus, Kazuko K., with Orani Dixon and Rosamund Weatherall. "Cross Country Data on Government Expenditure Classified by Functions." Studies in Domestic Finance no. 3, Development Economics Department. Washington, D.C.: World Bank, December 1973.

Banks, Baldwin R. C. "A Summary of Housing Finance Problems in Liberia." Monograph no. M/20. Copenhagen: U.N. Interregional Seminar on Financing of Housing and Urban Development, June 1970.

Brown, Jane Cowan. *Patterns of Intra-Urban Settlement in Mexico City: An Examination of the Turner Theory.* Dissertation Series no. 40. Ithaca, N.Y.: Cornell University, 1972.

Burns, Leland S. "Capital-Output Analysis of Housing Programs for Developing Nations." *Proceedings of the 7th Annual Meeting, Industrial Relations Research Association.* Edited by Gerald G. Somers. December 1964.

159

————. *Housing: Symbol and Shelter.* International Housing Productivity Study. Los Angeles: Graduate School of Business Administration, University of California, Los Angeles, 1970.

Carliner, Geoffrey. "Income Elasticity of Housing Demand." *Review of Economics and Statistics,* vol. 55 (November 1973), pp. 528–32.

Cockburn, Charles. *Construction in Overseas Development.* London: Overseas Development Institute, 1970.

Colombia, National Planning Office. *Aspectos Cuantitativos del Plan de Desarrollo.* Bogotá: National Planning Office, 1972.

————. *Investigación Socioeconómica de la Zona Oriental de Bogotá.* Bogotá: National Planning Office, May 1973.

Commonwealth Development Corporation. *Report and Accounts 1973.* London: Commonwealth Development Corporation, 1974.

Currie, Lauchlin. "Colombian Urban Policy in the Plan of Development." Bogotá: National Planning Office, 1974.

Davis, Kingsley. *World Urbanization 1950–1970.* 2 vols. Population Monograph Series no. 4. Berkeley, Calif.: University of California Press, 1969.

De Wilde, John C., and Associates. "A Framework for the Promotion of Construction Industries in the Developing Countries." World Bank Staff Working Paper no. 168. Washington, D.C.: World Bank, November 1973.

Dodge, J. Robert. *Cooperative Housing.* Ideas and Methods Exchange no. 52. Washington, D.C.: U.S. Department of Housing and Urban Development, 1971.

Eckaus, Richard. *Integration of Housing into National Development Plans.* New York: U.N. Center for Housing, Building and Planning, 1973.

Edmonson, Jack. *Report on the National Workshop on Low Cost and Cooperative Housing in Bangladesh.* Washington, D.C.: International Cooperative Housing Development Association, 1973.

Esroy, Turan. "Financing of Housing and Urban Development in Turkey." Monograph no. M/17. Copenhagen: U.N. Interregional Seminar on Financing of Housing and Urban Development, June 1970.

Figueroa, Adolfo, and Richard Weisskoff. "Viewing Social Pyramids: Income Distribution in Latin America." Paper presented at ECIEL Conference on Consumption, Income and Prices, Hamburg, West Germany, 1–3 October 1973.

Foundation for Cooperative Housing. *Cooperative Housing and the Minimum Shelter Approach in Latin America.* Washington, D.C.: Foundation for Cooperative Housing, 1972.

Fox, David J. "Patterns of Morbidity and Mortality in Mexico City." *Geographical Review*, vol. 62 (April 1972), pp. 151–85.

Frankenhoff, Charles. "The Economic Role of Housing in a Developing Economy." *Housing Policy for a Developing Latin Economy*. Rio Piedras, Puerto Rico: University of Puerto Rico, 1966.

————. "Elements of an Economic Model for Slums in a Developing Economy." *Economic Development and Cultural Change*, vol. 16 (October 1967), pp. 27–36.

Franklin, George H. "The Place of Housing in the National Plans of Developing Countries." Paper presented at International Congress, International Federation for Housing and Planning, Dublin, May 1969.

Geisse, Guillermo. *Notas sobre Renovación Urbana de Poblaciones Populares en Areas Metropolitanas*. Santiago: Universidad Católica, June 1970.

Grebler, Leo. "The Role of Housing in Economic Development." *Third World Congress of Engineers and Architects*. Tel Aviv: Association of Engineers and Architects in Israel, December 1973.

Grigsby, William G. *Housing Markets and Public Policy*. Philadelphia: University of Pennsylvania Press, 1963.

Grimes, Orville F., Jr. "Reappraising Urban Land Tax Effectiveness against Policy Goals." In *Urban Systems Research*. Edited by John W. Dickey and Roy W. R. Muncey. Report no. PB-241 120. Washington, D.C.: National Technical Information Service, April 1975, pp. 267–80.

————. "Urban Land and Public Policy: Social Appropriation of Betterment," World Bank Staff Working Paper no. 179. Washington, D.C.: World Bank, May 1974. Chapter 15 in *Local Service Pricing and Urban Spatial Structure*. Edited by Paul B. Downing. Vancouver, B.C.: University of British Columbia Press, forthcoming.

Grindley, W., and R. Merrill. *Sites and Services: the Experience and Potential*. Washington, D.C.: World Bank, May 1973; processed.

Hackenberg, Robert A. "The Poverty Explosion: Population Increase and Income Decline in Davao City, 1972." Davao: Davao Action Information Center, 1973; processed.

Halevi, Nadav. "Housing in Israel." In *Economic Problems of Housing*. Edited by A. A. Nevitt. New York: Macmillan, 1967.

Han, Ki Choon. "Capital-Output Ratio in Korea: A Trial." *Quarterly Economic Research*. Seoul: Economic Planning Board, 1964.

Harris, J. R. *Some Thoughts on a Housing Policy for Nairobi*. Discussion Paper no. 78. Nairobi: Institute for Development Studies, University College, 1969.

Hong Kong, Census and Statistics Department. *Hong Kong Population and Housing Census, 1971 Main Report.* Government of Hong Kong, Census and Statistics Department, 1972.

————. *1973/1974 Household Expenditure Survey.*

Howenstine, E. Jay. "Appraising the Role of Housing in Economic Development." *International Labour Review,* vol. 74 (January 1957), pp. 21–33.

Indian Statistical Institute. *The National Sample Survey, 19th Round: July 1964–June 1965,* no. 192. 1971.

Isbister, John. "Urban Employment and Wages in a Developing Economy: The Case of Mexico." *Economic Development and Cultural Change,* vol. 20 (October 1971), pp. 24–46.

Jakhade, V. M., and S. L. Shetty. "Distribution of Urban Household Wealth in India." *Economic and Political Weekly,* vol. 9 (May 1974), pp. 727–34.

Kenya, Ministry of Finance and Economic Planning. *Urban Household Expenditure Survey 1968–1969.* Nairobi: Ministry of Finance and Economic Planning, 1970.

Kenya, National Housing Corporation. "Records of Building and Infrastructure Costs." Nairobi: Nairobi City Council, 1970.

Kerala, Government of. *Performance Approach to Cost Reduction in Building Construction.* Report of Expert Committee. Trivandrum: Government of Kerala, January 1974.

Korea, Economic Planning Board. *Annual Report on the Family Income and Expenditure Survey.* Seoul: Economic Planning Board, 1970.

Lewis, K. J. *Income Distribution in Nairobi.* Nairobi: Nairobi Urban Study Group, March 1973.

Lewis, R. A. *Employment, Income and the Growth of the Barriadas in Lima, Peru.* Dissertation Series no. 46. Ithaca, N.Y.: Cornell University, 1973.

Lowry, Ira S., and others. *Rental Housing in New York City.* New York: New York City–Rand Institute, 1970.

Maisel, Sherman J. "Housing: Economic Aspects." *International Encyclopedia of the Social Sciences,* vol. 6. New York: Macmillan, 1968, pp. 521–26.

Mandelker, Daniel R. *Housing Subsidies in the United States and England.* New York: Bobbs-Merrill, 1973.

————, and Roger Montgomery. *Housing in America: Problems and Perspectives.* New York: Bobbs-Merrill, 1973.

Menezes and Partners. *Nairobi Eastern Extension, Report One.* Nairobi: Menezes and Partners, 1971.

Merrill, Robert N. *An Evaluation of Chile's Housing Program: Problems and Prospects.* M. A. thesis, Cornell University, June 1968.

――――. *Towards a Structural Housing Policy: An Analysis of Chile's Low Income Housing Program.* Dissertation Series no. 22. Ithaca, N.Y.: Cornell University, 1971.

Mexico, Secretaría de Indústria y Comercio. Dirección General de Muestreo. *Ingresos y Egresos de las Familias en la República Mexicana 1969–1970.* Mexico City: Secretaría de Indústria y Comercio.

Mohsin, Mohammed. "Institutional Financing of Housing Development in India." Paper no. 35, *Symposium on the Role of Housing in National Economy: Selected Papers and Reports.* New Delhi: National Building Organization, Government of India, and United Nations Regional Housing Centre (ECAFE), 1969.

Muth, Richard F. *Cities and Housing.* Chicago: University of Chicago Press, 1969.

Natarajan, B. *Economics of Housing in National Development.* Madras: Institute for Techno-Economic Studies, 1972.

National Council of Applied Economic Research. "Incidence of Taxation in Gujarat." New Delhi: National Council of Applied Economic Research, 1971.

Needleman, Lionel. *The Economics of Housing.* London: Staples Press, 1965.

Ness, Walter L., Jr. "Financial Markets Innovation as a Development Strategy: Initial Results from the Brazilian Experience." *Economic Development and Cultural Change,* vol. 22 (April 1974), pp. 453–72.

Nevitt, A. A. *Housing, Taxation and Subsidies.* London: Nelson, 1966.

Onibokun, Adepoju G. "Evaluating Consumers' Satisfaction with Housing: An Application of a Systems Approach." *Journal of the American Institute of Planners,* vol. 40 (May 1974), pp. 189–200.

Page, Alfred N., and Warren R. Seyfried. *Urban Analysis: Readings in Housing and Urban Development.* Glenview, Ill.: Scott, Foresman, 1970.

Perlman, Janice. *The Fate of Migrants to Rio's Favelas: The Myth of Marginality.* Ph.D. dissertation, Massachusetts Institute of Technology, 1970.

Plant, James S. "Family Living Space and Personality Development." In *A Modern Introduction to the Family.* Edited by Norman W. Bell and Ezra F. Vogel. Glencoe, Ill.: Free Press, 1960.

Pond, M. Allen. "The Influence of Housing on Health." *Marriage and Family Living*, vol. 19 (May 1957), pp. 154–59.

Reid, Margaret G. *Housing and Income*. Chicago: University of Chicago Press, 1962.

Rothenberg, Jerome. *Economic Evaluation of Urban Renewal*. Washington, D.C.: Brookings Institution, 1967.

Rush, Barney Sheppard. *From Favela to Conjunto: The Experience of Squatters Removed to Low-Cost Housing*. B.A. thesis, Harvard University, 1974.

Shah, S. P., and W. Schramli. "Prefabricated Construction in Industrially Developing Countries." *Proceedings of the Third International Symposium on Lower-Cost Housing Problems*. Edited by Oktay Ural. Montreal: May 1974, pp. 779–97.

Shibli, Khalid. *Housing: Short Range Tactics and Long Range Strategy*. Karachi: Planning Commission, Government of Pakistan, 1965.

Singapore, Housing and Development Board. *Annual Report 1972*. Singapore: Housing and Development Board, 1973.

Smith, Wallace F. *Housing: The Social and Economic Elements*. Berkeley, Calif.: University of California Press, 1970.

Soundararajan, V. "A Note on Income Distribution and Levels of Living in Tamil Nadu." Madras: State Planning Commission, 1971.

Stegman, Michael. *Housing Investment in the Inner City*. Cambridge, Mass.: M.I.T. Press, 1972.

Stone, P. A. *Urban Development in Britain: Standards, Costs and Resources 1964–2004*. Cambridge, England: Cambridge University Press, 1970.

Strassman, W. Paul. "Industrialized Systems Building for Developing Countries: A Discouraging Prognosis." *International Technical Cooperation Centre (ITCC) Review*, vol. 4 (January 1975), pp. 99–113.

————. "Innovation and Employment in Building: The Experience of Peru." *Oxford Economic Papers*, vol. 22 (July 1970), pp. 243–59.

————. "Measuring the Employment Effects of Housing Policies in Developing Countries." *Economic Development and Cultural Change* (forthcoming).

Streeten, Paul. *The Frontiers of Development Studies*. New York: John Wiley, 1972.

Sumintardja, Djauhari. "Lower Cost Housing Problems in Indonesia." *Proceedings of the Third International Symposium on Lower Cost Housing Problems*. Edited by Oktay Ural. Montreal, May 1974, pp. 690–706.

Tjioe, B. Khing, and Leland S. Burns. "Housing and Productivity: Causality and Measurement." *American Statistical Association, Proceedings of the Social Statistics Section,* 1966, pp. 155–60.

Turin, D. A. "Housing in Africa: Some Problems and Major Policy Issues." In *Economic Problems of Housing.* Edited by A. A. Nevitt. New York: Macmillan, 1967.

Turner, John C. "Housing Priorities, Settlement Patterns and Urban Development in Modernizing Countries." *Journal of the American Institute of Planners,* vol. 34 (November 1968), pp. 354–63.

United Nations. *Growth of the World's Urban and Rural Population, 1920–2000.* New York: United Nations, 1969.

———. "Report of the Secretary General on Proposed Fund for Human Settlements." New York: U.N. General Assembly Resolution 2999 (27), January 3, 1974.

———. *World Housing Survey.* New York: United Nations, 1974.

United Nations Industrial Development Organization. *Construction.* Monograph no. 2. Vienna: UNIDO, 1969.

U.S. Agency for International Development. *Guidance Statement on Urban Development.* Washington, D.C.: USAID, June 1973.

U.S. Department of Housing and Urban Development. *Special Report on Techniques of Aided Self-Help Housing.* Washington, D.C.: Government Printing Office, July 1973.

Ural, Oktay, editor. *Proceedings of the International Symposium on Low Cost Housing Problems Related to Urban Renewal and Development.* Rolla, Mo.: University of Missouri–Rolla, 1970.

Valenzuela, Jaime, and Georges Vernez. "Construcción Popular y Estructura del Mercado de Vivienda: El Caso de Bogotá." *Revista Interamericana de Planificación,* vol. 8 (September 1974), pp. 88–140.

Van Huyck, Alfred P. *Planning Sites and Services Programs.* Ideas and Methods Exchange no. 68. Washington, D.C.: U.S. Department of Housing and Urban Development, 1971.

Vernez, Georges. "Pirate Settlements, Housing Construction by Incremental Development and Low Income Housing Policies in Bogotá, Colombia." New York: New York City–Rand Institute, May 1973.

Wells, E. J., and E. R. Rado. *Constraints and Costs in the Kenya Building Industry.* Nairobi: University College, November 1968.

Western, John S., and others. "Housing and Satisfaction with Environment in Singapore." *Journal of the American Institute of Planners,* vol. 40 (May 1974), pp. 201–08.

Wilkinson, R. K. "The Income Elasticity of Demand for Housing." *Oxford Economic Papers,* vol. 25 (November 1973), pp. 361–77.

World Bank. *Urbanization Sector Working Paper.* Washington, D.C.: World Bank, June 1972.

————. *World Bank Operations.* Baltimore: Johns Hopkins University Press, 1972.

World Health Organization. "Appraisal of the Hygienic Quality of Housing and Its Environment." Technical Report no. 353. Geneva: WHO, 1967.

————. "The Physiological Basis of Health Standards for Dwellings." Public Health Paper no. 33. Geneva: WHO, 1968.

————. "Uses of Epidemiology in Housing Programmes and in Planning Human Settlements." Technical Report no. 544. Geneva: WHO, 1974.

Index

Abueva, José V., 23n
Advisory Commission on Intergovernmental Relations, 85n
Africa, 5, 12, 27–28, 37, 49, 58, 97
Ahmedabad, 8, 9; cost data for, 49, 80; construction costs and household income in, 76–77, 154–55; housing cost in, 69, 71, 81; land cost in, 43; service level in, 78
Akhtar, Sardar M., 28n
Ankara, 17
Araud, C., 33n, 85n
Architects' Combine, 51n
Arriaga, Eduardo E., 12n
Asia, 49

Bahl, Roy W., 12n
Bangladesh, 25, 104
Beirut, 13
Bell, Norman W., 46n
Bogotá, 8, 9, 62; building code in, 85; construction costs and household income in, 76–77, 152–53; cost data for, 49, 80; cost indexes of housing components in, 134; home income earning in, 37; housing cost in, 65, 69, 81; labor cost in, 52; land cost in, 43, 75; service level in, 78
Bombay, 26
Boon, G., 33n, 85n
Brazil, 52, 58
Brazzaville, 17
Brown, Jane Cowan, 48n, 49n
Building codes, 6, 15, 21, 84–85

167